Volume Five
American Tribal Religions

a monograph series,
published by the
Museum of Northern Arizona Press

Karl W. Luckert, General Editor
Department of Religious Studies
Southwest Missouri State University

WATERWAY

A Navajo Ceremonial Myth Told by Black Mustache Circle

Father Berard Haile, O.F.M.

Orthography by Irvy W. Goossen

Appendix by Karl W. Luckert

Museum of Northern Arizona Press

Manufactured in the U.S.A.

ISBN 0-89734-030-2
Library of Congress Catalog Card Number: 79-66605

Contents

WATERWAY

Introduction

The present account of the Waterway ceremonial of the Navajo was obtained in November, 1929, from *dághanáshjiin*, Black Mustache Circle, or for short, mustachy, *dághaaí* of *kįįłizhiní* (properly *kin dah łizhiní*, a black spot of a house) Black House, as the cornfields some eight miles northeast of Chinle, Arizona are called. His account of the Navajo Windway ceremonial is presented in a separate paper.[1] Taken as a whole, the present narrative is well told and the objective of a journey to a given locality is always some new acquisition of ritual paraphernalia. In his explanation of these details the informant has in this text been more fortunate than in his account of the Windway ceremonial.

The present ceremony belongs to the chantway series among Navajo ceremonials, and is not assigned to the *hóchǫ́ǫ́jí* group, or Ghostway ceremonials. In earlier days it was most likely performed as a major ceremonial, and efforts were always made to invite singers of this rite to corral dances of any description. A sandpainting is still made on rare occasions, as (formerly), when a boy and girl would imagine that the *alóól* or specialty of the *tóee*, which they had represented, had caused sickness. I found this painting in the Wheelwright collection.[2] Further details on such dancers *(alóól)* could not be obtained. In fact very little is heard of the ceremony today and, no doubt, it must now be classed among minor ceremonials which are only performed occasionally.

[1]The English version was published in Leland C. Wyman, *The Windways of the Navaho*, Colorado Springs, 1962.

[2]This apparently refers to the sandpainting which is given below in the Appendix as number five.

Undoubtedly, the disappearance of the ceremonial has been gradual and, as the informant stated, it is now largely confined to the cutting of prayersticks. With these particulars his account shows much familiarity and, fortunately, he has been able to give us many details of this phase in Navajo ritualism. He has also been able to present a fairly complete picture of the entire scheme of this vanishing ceremonial. Its connection with Hailway is suggested in the first part of the narrative, but details for comparison between the two ceremonials are not yet at hand. Similarly, the affinities with Downy Featherway are unmistakable.

On the other hand, its scheme is entirely distinctive. Water itself, water fowl, water animals and plants are brought to the foreground as a requisite for curing injuries inflicted by this basic element. Originally, venereal and skin diseases must have sought relief in this healing ceremonial. Evidently it overlapped to some extent with the Prostitutingway, as the story of the non-sunlight-struck Pueblo girls seems to indicate.[3] The informant, however, gives us no further details. Apparently the story is introduced to account for such prayer-sticks as those of Toad, of Spider, of Wrens and White Butterfly. Although, the relation of some of these to the element of water is distant.

Whatever the Water Monster may be, this personified being is made singer and author of the ceremonial and it is, apparently, typical of water's power to "draw persons into it" as its name implies. Dreams relating to "falling into the water" are ascribed to this being. Dreams that relate to drowning are ascribed chiefly to water horses, which seem to refer to water's power of holding its victim. This, however, is my own interpretation of the scant materials which are here presented.

At that, the informant is not offering us a complete account, but offers details with which he is familiar. These, as said, relate chiefly to the prayersticks.

For the translation and many additional suggestions we are indebted to Albert Sandoval of Lukachukai, Arizona.

Fr. Berard Haile, O.F.M.

Gallup, New Mexico
February, 1932

Fr. Berard Haile

[3]For Prostitutionway *(ajiłee)* see Father Berard Haile, *Love-Magic and Butterfly People*, American Tribal Religions, Volume 2; Flagstaff, 1978. The Deerway *ajiłee* was published in the same monograph series as Volume 3.

PART ONE: AN ENGLISH TRANSLATION

1. Riverward Knoll Woman and Scabby Woman

1. Concerning this Water ceremony way, it takes its beginning from the two old women who left the place called Riverward Knoll. One is called Riverward Knoll Woman, the other is the Scabby Woman, (and both) were in possession of means of knowing things. They obtained their knowledge through little winds of the kind that run about inside (of homes). Of these they owned two, one male the other female in kind, they say.

2. The one that went out from a place called Yucca Mountain was put in charge of it.[1] "You see, I am thinking of a different condition of things," she said, "and for this I shall ask for a certain person. You will perhaps see him," she said. So that Little Wind, the male one, was sent off above the sky. And he went up there. There, above the sky, he came to the Rainboy and to the Raingirl. When he reached them it happened that their home was made of dark cloud, and of blue cloud and of yellow cloud and of white cloud. They possessed zigzag lightning, and straight lightning, they possessed sunray and rainbow. There also happened to be a means by which knowledge was secured, the Dark Big Fly, the Blue Big Fly, the Yellow Big Fly, the White Big Fly, these were their means of knowing things.

3. So he (the messenger) it seems (said): "How will you be thinking about this?"[2] he said to Rainboy and Raingirl. He (Rainboy) spoke to one of those servants of his: "Run over to the east side (and) notify Dark Thunder," he told him. He came to him over there. And it happened that his home too was made of dark cloud, that zigzag

[1]While this renders the text as it stands accurately, the sense is that the two women were placed in charge of the one that came from Yucca Mountain. This is the Sunlight Boy of the story (Sandoval).

[2]That is, of the message which Little Wind brought them.

lightning was his entrance guard (and) that he lay there spraying water away from him. "I merely came to notify you that Rainboy asks you to come to him," he told him. He then started back and returned. "They are starting over from there," he reported. Again here on the south side[3] Blue Thunder happened to have a home of blue cloud with straight lightning for his door guard, and lay there spraying water away. He (the messenger) started out returning and returned saying: "They are starting out from there this way."

4. On the west side again he started out. Yellow Thunder, with a home of yellow cloud, had sunray for his door guard and lay there spraying water away from himself. Having started back again from there (the messenger) arrived returning with the report: "Presently they are coming this way from there." Again he started out on the north side, where White Thunder had a home of white cloud, rainbow for a door guard, and lay there spraying water away from himself. Having started out returning, he again arrived saying: "They are now on the way to here."

5. As for Dark Thunder, there was a means of his travel, he used Dark Wind in traveling. Blue Thunder had Blue Wind for his travel means; Yellow Thunder used Yellow Wind as a means of travel and White Thunder used White Wind. They came together (there). "Which (one) shall it be that shall return to Riverward Knoll?" he said. These Thunders, the four of them, were the ones who were discussing it.[4] "Which (of you) shall it be?" said Rainboy. Here they argued, they say, and decided upon sun's reflected ray,[5] in the form of a boy. "You are the one who must go down there, you must go to Riverward Knoll Woman," they told him. "All right," he said.

6. So after starting from here and, after rainbows had been crossed under his soles, he started going down there and came to the Riverward Knoll Woman. Her hogan,[6] he found, was made of white bead with a floor of white bead. Then, too, her hogan was of turquoise with a turquoise floor. Her hogan was of abalone with an abalone shell floor, her hogan was made of jet with a floor of jet. What he had seen

[3]Very likely the color of the Big Fly messengers corresponds to the color of the cardinal points.

[4]Or, if the address form of the text is retained, Rainboy tells the four Thunders: "discuss this (matter) who shall be selected."

[5]"Sun's temple red spots" denotes sunrays which pierce dark rain clouds. I have used "reflected sunray." In sandpaintings an oblong bar in rainbow colors is used to represent this.

[6]Her "home" could be used for "hogan."

of her hogan of jewels appeared to him only as such (he had imagined it). But when he looked closely, the place was very poor and had taken on its original form again.

7. And when he had moved just a little to the side, Big Fly Old Man came to him again. "Stay right here," he told him, "we will just await the outcome. I came for no special purpose, I simply wanted to inform you," he said to him. Four days had passed, he realized, while this had been discussed. "I wonder how it would be," said that Riverward Knoll Woman. "Somehow I have a notion (to go) to the place called Water Circle, I think we ought to go there," said the Riverward Knoll Woman. "This place, which is aside of the Wide Lake (area), I somehow have in my thoughts," she said.

2. The Home of Plants

8. At the time when August and September meet and vegetation is matured, they were discussing this. She happened to have a rainbow in her possession, which she threw out, and on top of this they went over to that place. One side was called Water Circle, the other Wide Lake, and at a point between them they stopped moving. When they had made camp there she at once said to him: "Go ahead, my Grandchild, go yonder to the Water Circle place." "For what purpose, my Grandmother?" he asked her. "Bring two (twigs) of blue (bark) willow and also two (twigs) of red (bark) willow," she told him. When he arrived there he cut them and returned with two blue and two red willow (twigs).

9. "Go again to the Wide Lake, my Grandchild," she said to him. "For what purpose, my Grandmother?" he asked. "Bring nine stalks of this (cattail) flag," she told him. And so it seems, he returned with these. They simply lay nearby. To that Wind by whom things became known to her she said: "Notify the people (to come) from yonder (to learn) how they will decide this for us," she told him. That male one started out eastward, came to the Bluebird People and brought them the news. That female one started out westward, came to the Pheasant[7] People and brought them the news. The Bluebird People

[7]The informant has not been questioned on this bird which the text calls *níłtsą́dlǫ́ǫ́'* (possibly "rain weasel"). A number of natives who have been asked seem to agree that a bird is meant, while others identify it with *náhádlǫ́ǫ́'*. This again is identified as a bird which can be seen in rainy seasons, by others as a creeping animal of the lizard family. My friend *hashké hayiyíídzį́į́s* of Lukachukai states that the late *adiłdiłí*, Stick Dice Gambler, assigned *níłtsą́dlǫ́ǫ́'* to the *ayáásh*, small birds. It is supposed to be drawn on by rain, is a pretty bird, of vari-colored and glittering plumage like a peacock, red eyes, a medium tail, similar to the roadrunner, but is not indigenous to the Navajo range. I have accepted this description to apply to the pheasant, and am using this in the translation.

(just) mentioned came in form of humans, those Pheasant People also came in form of humans, they say.

10. "It is just this. Of what (material) shall my hogan be (made)? For that purpose I am speaking, my Grandchildren," said Riverward Knoll Woman, and Scabby Woman too. "All right," they said. Coming from the east side those Bluebird People stopped and stood, and picked up the blue willow (twig) mentioned. Coming from the south side those Pheasant People picked up the red willow twig. Coming from the west side the Bluebird People picked up the other blue willow twig again. Coming from the north side the Pheasant People also picked up the other red willow twig. These were braced toward each other and with them the hogan was made. Along the east side the Bluebird People gathered the cattail flag mentioned, while the Pheasant People picked them up on the south side. In the west and north the same was repeated and all at the same time, they covered the hogan with that flag. After that, beautiful flowers were collected in the four directions. These were (laid) over the flag (stalks) all, without exception, with their tips downward and the hogan covered with them. This was done because, in this manner, the Rainside ceremony [8] must be (conducted). Thus the hogan was completed with the exit toward the east. "Thanks, now, my Grandchildren, you have built the hogan for me," she said.[9]

11. Distribution of jewels among them took place now. An offering of turquoise was given to the male Bluebird, and an offering of white shell beads to the female Bluebird. Then an offering of abalone shell was made to the male Pheasant and one of jet to the female one.[10]

[8] The sense is that the Waterway ceremony is conducted "for rain" at times. In this event all plants and flowers used in building the hogan for the ceremony are placed "tips downward." (Sandoval)

[9] Informant omitted the song at this point.

[10] This mentioning of the male and female birds indicates that they raised the poles of the hogan at each cardinal point, the male and female Bluebird in the east and west, the male and female Pheasant in the south and north. After that each one covered his side with flag and flowers, so that all four sides were completed "at the same time," as the text reads.

3. The Rough One, the Scrap Picker

12. Now it happened that there was a report: "Somewhat to the side of this Water Circle, towards the east side, the Hailway chant is to begin." It developed that Dark Thunder Man was to begin this sing. And when the old man (singer) was at the point of entering there, these over here, too,[11] were seated (living). Those two grandmothers of his were seated on the south side in the hogan, while he was huddled on the north side, having been made ugly for the time being. And so it seems that those Bird People who had come from yonder to build the hogan, had given him a name. Everyone called him the "Rough One." People also called him, "the one who picks up."[12] And so it seems, while he was huddled up on this side, opposite of him the two were huddled in a mat of slim grass. And at night they talked much about him, discussing his future (condition). And though he tried to understand, it was useless, because they spoke to each other in a whisper.

13. Dawn appeared and he was filled with anger. "What is this you are discussing that cannot be settled quickly! Both of you ought to be sleeping," he told them. "Hush! my Grandchild, don't say that! We were discussing what your future shall be," she told him. Everywhere there was daylight, still in places there were dark (shadowy) spots. "Although you may argue with us about it, my Grandchild, run around that mountain rice (plant) over there," she told him. "I should say not, I am lazy! What is the sense of running back and forth for no reason whatever!" he said. "Don't be saying that, my Grandchild, my babe. What you are to encircle is (in reality) horses,"[13] she told him.

[11]"Seated" is equivalent to "the place where they stayed." As this was the plant home, or ceremonial hogan, we can infer that the Water ceremony was being performed here, while the Hailway ceremony was in progress at the other place.

[12]"One who pecks" like a hen. "Scrap Picker" seems a good equivalent for one who searches the ash piles for scraps of food.

[13]Horses and sheep mentioned here are probably a later addition, and represent property in general (Sandoval). The narrative has no further reference to them. That property in general was probably meant originally, and was later replaced by horses and sheep with which the Navajo are now familiar, seems to be suggested by the soft goods and jewels in the third and fourth instances in which the hero is sent out.

4. She Dressed Him in Scabies

14. He ran around it, then came home. Directly it seems that Scabby Woman spoke: "Stand here, my Grandchild!" she told him. At once she dressed (covered) him with what is called scabies, and rubbed his surface with it.

15. (In the meantime the rite of fire-building was done over there.) His skin was covered completely, his lips turned inside out, his eyes as well. "Go ahead, now, go to the sing, my Grandchild! (Let us see) how much you will be ridiculed!" she told him. From there it seems he started immediately for that place. Towards the east of the place of the sing, the game of hoop and pole was being played. It happened that the *yé'ii* people were hoop-poling,[14] that the small Bird People were hoop-poling. Talking-god's hoop and pole was a white shell bead, Calling-god was hoop-poling with turquoise. At the hoop-poling goal he sat down in the awful condition he was in. "Whoever thinks of sitting at the hoop-pole goal in such a condition! Be gone from there! Get away, you are simply (too) ugly (for anything)!" they were saying to him. On this account he simply bowed his head. He made no reply. From there he started out and came again toward the west side, where the cooking was being done. Bluebird maidens, Yellowbird maidens, Blue Swallow maidens, speckled Yellowbird maidens, *nahoodlǫ́ǫ́*[15] maidens, Pheasant maidens, Turtledove maidens, that many were occupied with food preparations.

16. These same people[16] were hoop-poling at the other place. On his account these would not come (to the kitchen), being repulsed by the sight of him. "How, I wonder, can I go again to the sing place? It is evident that people avoid me," he thought. "I shall tell my grandmother, let her know about this," he thought. Immediately he started returning to his hogan. Late in the afternoon he arrived, returning. "Return and stand in the center, my Grandchild," the Scabby Woman said to him. She had arrived from the east gathering herbs, the flowers

[14] "Hoop-poling" is a convenience form for "playing the game of hoop and pole."

[15] The House Builder suggests that *nahoodlǫ́ǫ́'* is a yellow breasted weasel used in the mountain chant for unravelings (*wooltáád* bundles) and neck scarves (*zeedeelyé*). But, evidently, this description will not fit in this gathering of birds.

[16] That is, the menfolk of these Bird People.

of all of which she had plucked. With these she rubbed him. All the sores, with which he had been covered, fell from him, they say.

17. *Riverward Knoll Woman at Riverward Knoll, scabies I have made your sacrifice,*
A pretty white bead[17] *I have made your sacrifice!*
Pretty iron ore I have made your sacrifice, pretty blue pollen I have made your sacrifice, pretty pollen I have made your sacrifice!
(Therefore) take your magic out of me again! You have taken your magic out of me again!
Start out carrying it away from me again! You have carried it far away from me again!
Let him nicely recover! Let him nicely walk out!
Let him nicely walk about! Let him go about with nothing to prevent him! Let him go about immune to all sickness!
Let him go about with a pleasant path before him!
Let him go about with a pleasant path behind him!
Let him go about as one who is Long-life, as one who is the Happiness One!
Pleasant it has become again! Pleasant it has become again![18]

18. Up to there it happened so. On the second night of the ceremony he was huddled together in the same place again, and his grandmothers opposite him were again in conversation about him, although he could not get the drift of it. When dawn appeared in the distance he again argued with them about it. "What is all this talk about? For goodness sake, go to sleep!" he told them. "Don't be saying that, my Grandchild," she said to him. But he again spoke to them: "Yesterday the people never ceased to ridicule me. Whatever it was you clothed me with, the people did not cease to laugh at me," he told them. "Still you must not talk that way, my Grandchild. We were (just) discussing your future condition," she told him. "Now run around that gray greasewood over there!" she told him. "But I am sleepy now, I am lazy," he said to her. "Even so, if you run around it, it is (in reality) sheep, my Grandchild," she told him.

[17] The sequence of jewels in the narrative is white bead, turquoise, abalone, jet, which is to be observed here in the prayers for Spanish pock, itch by dragon's head sage, and by nettle.

[18] Repeated by the patient the forms should be changed, for instance, "Let me recover nicely, at my front, etc." The informant uses the polite forms of address, which is not the customary form used by the women in addressing the hero. The same prayer is repeated after each disease with which he is afflicted, excepting that, in the second and fourth prayers, "rear and front" are mentioned instead of the "front and rear" sequence of the first and third prayers.

5. She Covered Him with Spanish Pock

19. So he encircled that and returned from there as dawn appeared. "Stand again in the center (of the hogan)," she told him, and when he again stood there she clothed him with Spanish pock. "Now go over there again, my Grandchild. Let them laugh at you again," she told him. He again came over there where hoop-poling was done. At the hoop-pole goal he again sat down. And so, being in this awful shape, he sat there simply with his head bowed. "Get out of here! Walk on! Rough One! Scrap Picker! They may hoop-pole you!" they said to him. From there he started off again and came again to the place where food was being prepared. "What can be done about it! He continues to come to us, simply ugly as he is! Go away! Don't continue coming to us!" it was said to him.

20. "Let me see, why is it that people hate me so," thinking this he proceeded towards the sing place. Along the entrance he came and stood. Something called a sewed fabric happened to be the entrance curtain. This he raised at the south side, and there, in the rear part of the hogan lay the singer, while this way others were sitting. "What can be done with it! That must be he of whose presence there is talk. Tell him to get away, by all means!" said he who was the singer. "I wonder why he says that," he thought. When he was about to express himself in this manner he again raised the other side (of the curtain), but (noticed) his twelve wives who had their heads bowed on his account.[19]

21. Immediately it seems he started returning and returned yonder, where his grandmothers were, in the late afternoon. The flowers of nice plant tips she had again gathered, from the south. With these she again rubbed his skin and all sores fell from him. When

[19]The meaning is apparently that he checked himself and said nothing when he noticed the twelve women through the opening in the curtain.

these had disappeared from him she spoke to him: "What was said to you, my Grandchild?" she asked. "What would be said to me anyway! People now have simply ridiculed me for good! People enjoyed a (good) laugh at my expense! That's clear!" he told her. "Be it so, my Grandchild. Be patient for some time, and we shall see! Go now and don't worry, (but) sleep!" she told him. And having directly returned to (his) place, he again huddled together.

22. Then the night passed while on their side they talked about him. He did not get the drift of it. When dawn had appeared in the distance he again upbraided them: "What can be done about it! What are you so busy talking about? Go to sleep! On your account (can't you see!) I am breaking my sleep off and on, I cannot sleep!" he told them. "Shoo! my Grandchild. Don't say that! We were discussing your future condition," she said to him. "That may be, but people simply laugh at me, laughter at my expense makes them happy, that's all!" he said to them. "Don't say that, my Grandchild, (but) run again, around that piñon tree," she said to him. "And if I should run around it, what would I acquire?" he said to her. "Oh! that is soft goods, my Grandchild," she told him. (So) around it he ran and returned (to them). "Now come and stand in the center (of the hogan), my Grandchild," she then told him. "Let them now laugh at you! We shall see what comes of it, my Grandchild," she said.

6. She Clothed Him in Dragon's-head Sage

23. With dragon's-head sage[20] she again clothed him. "Let us see! Go over there again, my Grandchild, go ahead!" she told him. After his skin was covered again, he again left there and went to the place where they were hoop-poling and sat down there. "What can be done with this thing! He has come to us again, ugly as he is! Go away from here (for goodness sake!) Rough One! Scrap Picker! Don't be continually coming to us!" again was said to him, "they may hoop-pole you." He simply sat there with bowed head. And directly starting away from there, he came to the food-preparing place. "What shall be done (with it). The simply ugly one has come to us again," they too said of him. From there he just proceeded to the sing place where he passed by the entrance, (and) returned to the place where his two grandmothers were staying.

24. "Stand again in the center of the hogan, my Grandchild," she told him. The tips of beautiful flowers in the west she had again collected, and she applied these to him. Again (the sores) fell from him. "Yes?, my Grandchild, what has again been said about you? How was the discussion about you again?" she asked him. "There is no doubt about it, people just ridicule me, people just poke fun at me, they make a nice laughter about me!" he answered her again. "Be it so, my Grandchild, we shall see how it will turn out! Go to sleep again over there," she told him.

25. Again he lay down over there (while) opposite him his grandmothers huddled facing each other. And then the two began to busy themselves with talk and the night passed along while they spoke about him. At dawn he spoke to them again: "What is it anyway! You sure are great ones! Even sleep you disregard! Go to sleep, (for goodness sake!) On your account I do not sleep well," he told them. "Shoo! my Grandchild, did I not tell you not to speak that way? Be patient, my Grandchild, we will see what will come of it!" she told him. "At any rate, run around that cedar again," she said. "But sleep is (so) sweet (and) I am lazy!" he told her. "Anyway, run again now, my Grandchild, my babe," she said to him. "But if I should run around it, what is it (in reality)?" he asked her. "Don't talk, my Grandchild, it is jewels," she told him. He encircled that juniper (cedar) and returned again. Immediately she said, "Come here and stand in the center (of the hogan), my Grandchild."

[20] Or rather, with the eczema which this plant produced.

7. She Covered Him with Nettle

26. When she again rubbed his skin with nettle, his skin was again much covered (with sores). "Try that again! Go over there again to the hoop-poling, to the sing," she said to him. "This time you shall not sit down at the hoop-poling place, (but) walk around everywhere among them. Also, where they are preparing the food, you shall go everywhere among them. Then you will (also) enter the sing place," she said to him. Leaving here he then again arrived over there. They again began to laugh about him and to poke fun at him. Even so he walked among the people (who) ran away on his account. He entered the sing place (and) pretended to sit down almost, (when) those women all sat down with their backs turned to him. So at once it seems he proceeded to leave there and late in the afternoon he returned home. "Walk up to the center and stand there, my Grandchild," she said to him.

27. The flowers of beautiful plant tips from the north she had collected. With these she rubbed his skin from which all (sores) again fell off. "Yes? my Grandchild. What has been said to you again?" she asked him. "This time people simply poked fun at me, people had a pretty laugh on me," he told her. "All right, my Grandchild, I see, so it is. Now, although conditions be such, (and), although there be one by whom he knows things, the Dark Big Fly shall not become aware of it."

28. Shortly after noon the Little Wind, already mentioned, was sent out in the direction toward the east. Dark Wind was notified. "Although it is (true) that I possess baskets, mine shall not (be used). She herself possesses some, she, the Riverward Knoll Woman." This message Little Wind brought back. "Sure I possess some," said she and started off eastward. That woman herself, it developed, had dug out soaproot, the width of four fingers in size. So then a sewed fabric was spread out, on top of which that soaproot was kneaded. With this he bathed himself completely, and with white (bead) shell he was dried, they say.

8. He Committed Adultery with the Singer's Wives

29. After that his grandmother, who was second in rank, again made spreads of sewed fabric here, on top of which white shells were placed. "Lie down prone now on top of that sewed fabric," she told him. She then stretched his limbs, putting his muscles, too, in (good) shape. With her hands she stretched his hair out clear down to his thigh. She clothed him in white shell. A perfect (bowl of) white shell she set on top of his head. Ramming them downward, she pressed white shell beads into his hair. As a young man he arose, glittering all over he arose. "Directed by these now (their suggestion), you will be going about, my Grandchild, my babe," was said to him. At either side little winds, already mentioned, were placed into his earfolds. "As for me, I too am likewise provided for, my Grandchild. I suppose you will do this and that to him, for this purpose this is (arranged for you)," she told him.

30. Meanwhile the first full-night sing was in progress over there. "Go on, my Grandchild, go over there! Perhaps on your account they will bow their heads again. On your account they will perhaps shy away again!" she said to him. From there he proceeded to that place. The Holy People and (small) Bird People, women too, had gathered in great numbers. There he arrived and walked about outside. They put their heads into each others ears (whispering): "What strange man is this that came? He is just embarrassingly (attractive)," they were saying. From there he entered (and) when an opening had been made for him the space was provided for him behind the singer's seat. They would not look at him, on his account they continued with bowed heads, they felt embarrassed in his presence. They say, that his (the singer's) wives were very pretty. These entered. Off and on while looking at him they would smile. Directly the basket was turned (to face) down. The first night singing was done.[21] The basket was

[21]That is, the first night of tapping the basket, which is the fifth of a nine-night ceremonial, or the first of a five-night ceremonial (Sandoval).

turned up. When he started to go outside from there the surplus[22] two had gone out to follow him. With these he slept each in turn, and in this way it came to be that he did adultery to that singer.

31. He returned to where his grandmothers were (sitting). "How is it, Grandchild?" she asked. "I committed adultery with the singer's wives," he said. "That's exactly as I said (intended) it to be, my Grandchild," she told him. After that a sewed fabric was spread out for him upon which he lay down. Another was spread over him after he had removed the jewels from himself. The night passed with them, sleeping only.[23] When dawn appeared in the distance she told him: "Run (there) and back again, my Grandchild." Around the same mountain rice again he ran. Having returned he was again bathed in a turquoise basket with wide-leaf yucca, and also dried with turquoise.

32. When this had been done to him he went about right around there just keeping things holy for himself,[24] till it began to be late in the afternoon. He was again dressed up in that turquoise, as said. "Go over there now again, my Grandchild," she told him. Again he arrived over there and simply stood around nearby on the outside (of the hogan). In the same way they again whispered to each other. When an opening had been made for him he again entered. Space was again provided for him (right) behind the singer's place, where he sat down as before. Those wives (of the singer) were again grouped on the opposite side. Immediately the basket was turned down again (for) the second night's singing. When the basket was turned up again he left to return. Three ran after him. With these three he spent the night, (and thus) in two nights he had thrown five.

33. Immediately he started to return from there and again returned to his grandmothers. "What have you done there, my Grandchild?" she again asked him. "I committed adultery with the singer's wives. I slept with three of them, no doubt about it," he said. "That is good! That is exactly what you are to do. For that purpose I am your instructor, my Grandchild," she told him. Immediately something called "white streaks over its surface"[25] was again spread out for him. He undressed (and) simply spent the night on it. On the other side, too, his grandmothers again spent the night.

[22]The "surplus two" or the "two above ten" of the twelve wives.

[23]That is, nothing more was undertaken that night.

[24]"Keeping things holy" probably refers to the bath and drying and remaining at home. By some magic the grandmothers had concealed the actions of their grandchild from Big Fly, the spy of the singer. His stay at home, therefore, would arouse no suspicion (Sandoval).

[25]This seems to have been a black and white fabric. The name suggests that the white streaks were sewn on the black base, and were undoubtedly of Pueblo origin.

34. At dawn she told him: "Now run again along yonder, my Grandchild." Again he ran around gray greasewood as he had run the first time, and returned again. As it was done the first time in that same way it was done again. He was again bathed with slim yucca in an abalone basket and dried again with abalone shell. After simply walking about around there (till) pretty late afternoon, he was again dressed in abalone shell. Immediately he started out again for the third night singing. He came over there again and simply walked nearby among the people. From here again he entered and space was again made for him in back of the singer. Now up to this time his doings had not been noticed, they say. The (singer's) wives all entered again. That basket was again turned down, and from yonder they were smiling at him. The basket was turned up again. When they started to go out he again followed them (and) it happened that three of them left to follow him.[26] With each one of these he again slept.

35. Then he again returned yonder to his grandmothers, as before. "Yes? my Grandchild, what have you done again?" she asked him. "I again committed adultery with the singer's wives, of course," he said. "That is what you are to do! That's the object, my Grandchild, my babe," said that old woman. At once a dark sewed fabric was again spread out for him here, on which he undressed and on which he also passed the night. His grandmothers, too, spent the night again in that same place and no further details were mentioned to one another.

36. "Go ahead now, my Grandchild, run again," he was told at dawn. As on the first occasion, he again ran around a piñon. When he again returned from that, a jet basket was again placed down for him, soap was again prepared with which he was bathed, and he was dried again with jet. After that a white robe was spread out for him again, on which he was dressed with jet. By that time the fourth night singing was on over there. He again proceeded to go there and arrived, but simply stood near the entrance. Directly he entered, a space was made for him again over there by the side of the singer. The women again entered on their side. (After the singing) the basket was again turned up. When all the menfolk of those Bird People had again gone out, the women filed out after them, and he started after them. Two of them again ran after him. With these he slept again.

37. And from there it seems he again returned to his grandmothers. "What have you done, my Grandchild?" she asked. "I have committed adultery with the singer's wives," he said. "Those who were giving you any old name. Those who used to call you the Rough One, who used

[26]The text reads, "when the (people) left again, he also followed them out, three also happened to leave behind him."

to call you the Scrap Picker, who are not your equals, these you have thrown down," said his grandmother to him. "One more time (still) remains, my Grandchild, my babe! Now go to sleep here!" she told him. And so it seems he simply passed another night.

38. "Go ahead, run again my Grandchild, once more remains (to be done)," she told him at dawn. Around that cedar again he ran. When he returned he was not bathed again, what is called sunlight pollen only was applied to him. "You have now done the full amount," she said. That is, so far as repeated running was concerned, the full amount was completed. So it seems, that over there the close (of the ceremony, "its day") was being held. And when this time only sunlight pollen had been applied to him, he went about in this way till in the late afternoon, when this time he was clothed in every kind of those jewels mentioned.

39. At once he left for that place while it was still daylight. Now over there the Holy People had gathered in great numbers. And so, when he went among them, they made room for him (wherever) he went. They felt embarrassed on his account, people did. The sun set, but he still went about right around there. He would go inside, he would go out (as he liked). And it seems that for some time, the singing did not begin. But after a while the basket was turned down again. This time the singing continued all night long. During the time that the singing was on, he would sit down just for that short period, while otherwise his work[27] on the outside was tiring him, he was night-traveling, and slept with the (two) remaining ones. When he had thrown the twelve, the ceremony was ended. When the dawn songs were begun, that Wind told him: "He has seen you! Before daylight falls on you, you must leave to return to your grandmothers," he said. He ran to his grandmothers for safety. "'You have been seen by the person!' the Little Wind told me," he said. "In what manner shall it be, Grandmother? Whatever you have decided let that happen to me. Perhaps you will turn me over to the people?" he said. "Yes, how shall it be, Grandchild! Much as I wish, there is no place to put you aside," she said. And so it seems, (for) that day the sun set.

[27]What this work was is expressed in the following: "He was night-traveling," which is the common expression for sexual intercourse.

9. The One Whose Home is of Down

40. "This coming dawn an attack will be made on us," that night the Little Wind told him. "Shall I perhaps start off this way? Here, on the shore of the Wide Lake perhaps, I shall be spared I think," he said. "Wonder how you think of it for me?" he said to her. And so it seems this (same) night his two grandmothers were seated at the exit, one on either side. That night it seems passed, with them on the lookout there for him (for the enemy). When dawn appeared in the distance, his grandmother gave him a rainbow, and at once he started off toward the shore of Wide Lake. Suddenly along where he had just left, a noise broke out. What (follows) now was for the purpose of giving him another name. Following him from over there the people gave chase in order to kill him, on either side they ran, some were behind him. Coming this way the people started tracking him, and they tracked him to the shore of Wide Lake. Then it seems he threw out a rainbow upon the water surface. On this he walked out yonder to the center of the water (where) he went into a bunch of coarse grass. The rainbow he pulled toward himself, (and) it jumped into that place after him. The coarse grass mentioned he laid below himself, crossing it, and upon this he sat down. And so, it seems, while he was sitting down in there, along over here the people, spreading out in a mass, overtook him, as his tracks lead right to the water edge and no farther. From there they uselessly spread out on either side around the lake, continuing their vain efforts until sunset. "Wonder what has become of him! Maybe he has gone down to the water bottom," they were saying this merely within his hearing.

41. After sunset all had left. Now, finally, he raised himself in the interior of that coarse grass, then looked around from there, but no one was in sight. He scanned in vain. From there he again threw the rainbow across. "Now proceed to return on it, they have all left, they are just talking about you over there," said that Little Wind to him

from his earfolds. He returned to his grandmothers in the night. "Where is it that you were missed, my Grandchild, my babe?" she said to him. "Don't oversleep by any chance, my Grandchild, be sure to remain conscious (sleep lightly)," she said. On either side of the exit the two sat keeping watch over him, right here he passed the night.

42. "Get up, my Grandchild, it is dawn," she said. "Now go again to that same place, only at that place there is safety, at the Wide Lake," she said. She (then) stepped to the rear part of the hogan, she who was first in rank did this. She happened to have a dark bow and a tail-feathered arrow in her possession, which she gave him. "Now you will go again to the shore of Wide Lake. There you will make your hogan of willows and then do killing (game) with these," she told him. That (having been told him), he started out for that place. There he constructed his hogan of willows just large enough for himself, and covered it with beautiful flowers.

43. He was sitting inside, when from all sides noises were heard. And it happened that, from the very entrance out at the water edge, a flock of bridled titmice had gathered in a circle, and from there started toward the water, some were still coming on from yonder. At once he grabbed that dark bow and the tail-feathered arrow, and shot one of them over there. He (then) grabbed another (arrow), called "yellow tail-feathered", and shot another (bird) with it. They moved on away from him. He picked up those arrows which (he) had dispatched and also those (birds) he had killed, and brought them inside of the hogan. He plucked (their feathers) completely, both of them (giving him) that much of a (small) heap of feathers. Some half round flag stood along the shore, of which he plucked some. He (then) dug a trench just his size into which he laid that bevel-edged flag. Upon this he placed the downy feathers and at sunset lay down in them.

44. When dawn appeared yonder, "Again it is getting fierce (dangerous)! From yonder the people are now preparing another attack on you," that Little Wind spoke to him along his temples. "Now get into the rough grass again, and with the rainbow throw yourself into the water again. It is getting to be fierce now again along there!" he said. He threw out the said rainbow, on top of which he walked, went into the rough grass again as before, and behind himself he again drew that rainbow toward himself. That coarse grass again he laid across in a bundle and sat down upon it. The crowd of people again overtook him: "Evidently here he had his hogan. It is clear that he spends the night inside this down. What has become of him, of Hogan-of-Down?" it was said. Again a fruitless search was made for him everywhere along the shore. In vain the search for him went on till again the sun set. Again, after sundown, he stood upon the rainbow

as before. Crossing over on it, he again went to the hogan he had made and again spent the night inside those plumes as previously.

45. At dawn Little Wind said to him, "Arise! Look toward the east!" he was told. In that direction he turned his gaze when (behold) black clouds in the form of beautiful, keystone-shaped clouds, were set one on top of the other. Along its top, Dark Wind was standing. "Again turn your eyes southward!" he was told. And there blue clouds, in the form of two keystone clouds, were set one above the other. On top of these Blue Wind again was standing. "Turn your eyes westward again," he was told. And there yellow clouds, in the form of two keystone clouds, were set resting upon one another, on top of these Yellow Wind was standing. "Northward turn your eyes again," he was told. And here white clouds, in form of two keystone-shaped clouds, resting upon each other, were set. On top of these White Wind was standing.

46. That one in the east said to him: "Now then, what is there that can harm you! Now (it is settled that) you are my child, you are my Grandchild," he said. The one in the south, that Blue Wind, spoke likewise to him. That Yellow Wind from the west likewise spoke to him. From the north that White Wind also spoke likewise to him. At that time he also took him, among others, into his care: "You will act according to instructions from your grandmothers," Black Wind told him. "And, as for this fact of missing (sparing) you, you are (fully) aware of the cause of this which is being done to you," he said. "Eventually it will come upon you, so it is ordained, even though this time (you are spared), my Grandchild," he told him. "You see, you have in your possession the means by which you are informed of things," he said. "Although it is known that in this manner he (your enemy) has power, still all will be on the surface (and not harm you)," he said.

10. Rainbow Arrived with Him in the Skies

47. "Now go and return to your grandmothers," he said. "When it is known that what the two speak to you again is the best thing to do, you shall start out again in accordance with (their words)," he said. "All right I shall now return over there," he replied. He returned where his (two) grandmothers were sitting. "You have realized it, I suppose, my Grandchild, my babe!" she said to him. "Who is it, do you think, my Grandchild, that has told you?" she asked him. "That is the Dark Cloud, it's the Dark Wind, he it is that told me, I am positive," he said. "According to whose mind did this happen, do you think, my Grandchild?" she asked. "'Yours, of course', tell her," said Little Wind from his earfolds. "Yours of course, according to the mind of you two this was done, my Grandmothers," he said to them. "That is very true," she said. "As for what you have done to him, eventually it will come upon you, so it is ordained, my Grandchild," she told him. She referred to the adultery which he had committed.

48. "At daylight, just when the sun is coming up, you will proceed to the center of Wide Lake and stand there," she said. "When you (thus) have taken your position there, you will cross the rainbow under your soles. That one will rise with you," she said. "It will take you yonder above the skies, and when it has arrived with you, some time or other, we two will overtake you there. That is the plan, my Grandchild," she told him. That (done) he spent the night right there.

49. And directly after starting off from there, he came to the center of the lake and stood there. That rainbow (pair) he crossed, heads in opposite directions, under his soles. In the direction eastward that water began to move. When it had done likewise on the south side it moved somewhat higher up with him. When it again had moved on the west side, it went way out of reach and moved higher with him. When it had done likewise again on the north side, it rose quite a

distance with him. All around the center (the whole lake) moved its waves back and forth.

50. When that happened he came up inside through the skyhole. People were there also, he found. A sing was (in progress). Outside the uprights were set in place,[28] they say. These uprights got angry with him.[29] Sandpaintings kept them occupied when he entered. Over there, by the side of the singer, a place was made for him. It turned out to be a Waterway chant and Water Monster Old Man was the singer. "Whence do you come, my Grandchild? Around here earth surface people are not allowed," he said (to him). "I can go anywhere," he said. "(But) I am from Water Circle, I come from Wide Lake, you must know," he said.

51. The making of a sandpainting was in process. Rainboy did the leading, they say, and Duck Young Men happened to be busy with it. Non-flying Duck Young Men (mud-hens), these also; Jacksnipe Young Men too; Dowitcher Young Men too; Curlew Young Men (twigbill?) also; (American) Bittern Young Men also; Roundbill Crane Young Men also; Snowy Egret Young Men also; Crane *nahabił* Young Men also; (Speckled?) Crane Young Men also; Grouse Young Men also; *tó níłhę̨shii* Young Men also; Sandhill Crane People Young Men, the Chief of (all of) them, also; Thunder Young Men also; these, it seems, he saw being busy with the sandpainting.

52. And Old Man Toad was supervising it, he was giving orders for it. Greenfrog Young Men, Minnow Young Men, Tadpole Young Men, Beaver Young Men, Otter Young Men, (Water) Turtle Young Men, (Land) Turtle Young Men, Waterdog Young Men, Rattlesnake-with-the-white-forehead Young Men, Watersnake Young Men, Flying Snake (?) Young Men, their Chief; that many were included. And the females of everyone of these (should be) added. And so, it seems, (the ceremony was performed and) the sandpainting was erased in his presence. In the night the basket, too, was turned down in his presence. After his arrival the basket was turned down three times in his presence. When the closing day (of the ceremony) arrived, the sun went down again while he was present there (taking it all in). It came about that he was learning (without realizing it).

53. About that time his (two) grandmothers overtook him. "Did you really overtake me, my Grandmothers?" he said to them. "Yes,

[28]The uprights are plumes, wide boards, medicine spoons and stoppers, which are set on improvised mountains outside. After the sandpaintings are finished inside the hogan, these uprights are set around along the border of the painting.

[29]Or perhaps, not exactly angry. They gave some warning to those inside of the advent of the stranger (Sandoval). Nothing more is added in the text to explain this remark.

my Grandchild, we did overtake you," she said (to him). Over there door guards were appointed. On the south side (of the entrance) Rattlesnake was made to sit, on the other (the north) side Watersnake (was) placed, (while) Dark Big Fly was found at the juncture of the poles. His (two) grandmothers entered (and) a place was provided for them on the south side. While they were white-haired old women at the time he had left them over there, he found that now they had become young maidens. Old Man Water Monster happened to be their granduncle (mother's father's brother). On his side they were his grandchildren. From their side Rainboy was their grandchild, on his side they were his grandmothers. And so here the relationship became known. There then he realized it all around, (the) Down Hogan (Man) did. And so it happened, they say.

11. Sunlight Boy

54. "Now continue on the lookout all night long" was said to Dark Big Fly by Old Man Water Monster and Rainboy. The Old Man Water Monster again spoke. "As for you who are the door guards, you too will be on the lookout," he told them. Rainboy again spoke. "That, I am sure, is the only good way to continually be on the lookout," he said to them. "All right, we shall do so," both of them said. You see, over at Riverward Knoll he came down. From there he went to Water Circle and then to Wide Lake. Here between (these) two places, going back and forth, he was disrespected by them. Rough One they called him, Scrap Picker they called him, a little later Down Hogan he was called. But here finally he was called what he really is, by his true name, Sunlight Boy he was called. "Over this one you will keep watch, for that purpose you will be on the lookout," Old Man Water Monster told them.

55. "Watching out for the Thunder People (must) continue," he said. "Dark Thunder who is their chief and lies on the east side is no good," he said. "And Blue Thunder lying on the south side, who is their chief, is no good," he said. "The one lying on the west side, Yellow Thunder who is their chief, is no good," he said. "Below the north, White Thunder who is their chief, is no good," he said. "And Left-handed Wind is no good," he said. "Spotted Wind is no good," he said. "The one called Left-handed Thunder, and the one called Spotted Thunder is no good," he said. After these instructions had been completed, the spies for those places had (thus) been appointed. "All right, we shall be on the lookout as best we can," they said.

56. In the meantime the Transparent Stone Boys from the Sun's home had arrived. Over here, right by his side, space was provided for them. That Old Man Water Monster said: "Where from are you, my Grandchildren?" he asked. "We (came) from the Sun's home, you see," they said. Now it seems that to this door guard, who was on the south side, an offering was made of white bead shell, to the one on the north side an offering of white haliotis was made.[30] "For what purpose did

[30]This mentioning of the offerings made to the door guards seems out of order at this point. It was probably forgotten at the time when their appointment was mentioned, it overlooks Big Fly at the smokehole. White haliotis is a white conch with an admixture of red, according to native informants.

you come my Grandchildren?" he said. "You see, although you are powerful in this way, how is it that you are performing (the ceremony) with something missing?" he asked. "What in particular is it, my Grandchildren?" he asked.

57. He reached under his arm and brought from there what is called *náhálnih biyázhí*.[31] "You see, if this is available, only then may one sing the Waterway," he said. Talking Prayerstick it is called, they say. "Now then, you can finish your singing with strength, my Granduncle," he told him. "Put it in a basket over there in the rear part of the hogan, only then can it not be taken (away) from you," it was said to him. "Now inhale its breath," he was told. In accordance with this we singers now do it in this manner. "What you are now doing (is well enough), but some people are unaware of it, they have not been present," he said. "Where is there one man that does not know of it? The fact is, it has become known everywhere," he (the Water Monster) said. "It is not so (even though) you say so," he told him. (For instance), where you now proceed to close this (chant), with what will you close it?" he was asked. "Well, it will simply close with the same line (of songs) as are in progress. Why is it that you say this, my Grandchildren?" he said.

58. "Even so, it is not as you say. The particular thing which is given to you, the Sun has given us (and), in order that now nothing shall be omitted, it lies over there. Should the omission take place it cannot be called the close of the singing," he said. "All right, my Grandchildren, I did not know this. But where is he who will finish it? You speak of this as though it were known to you, my Grandchildren," he said. "We certainly know it, we do," said the Transparent Stone Boys. "On the summit of *sisnaajiní* there are the Bluebird People Young Men. These must, of course, do the finish of the singing," he (they) said. "The Blue Swift-people Young Men, at the summit of Mount Taylor, they are it, of course, who must finish the ceremony at dawn," he said. "The Speckled Yellow Bird People Young Men, at the summit of the San Francisco Peaks, these, of course, must do the finish singing," he said. "The Cornbeetle People Young Men of Perrin's Peak summit will do the finish singing, of course," he said. To this extent the command was given, they say. To the one sitting at the pole joints it was said: "Go ahead, Dark Big Fly, make the rounds!" He left and returned in a very short time saying: "'All right,' they said, 'we will be there at dawn.'" "All right, I see, that is the way it is," said Water Monster and Rainboy also.

[31] This has not been identified. Someone has suggested a plume. The "talking prayerstick" with which the text identifies it, does not give us an equivalent for *náhálnih*, especially in the combination with "its offspring or child."

12. Closing of the Waterway Ceremony

59. At once the basket was turned (upside) down, around which all who were there crowded. "Going outside is not allowed," was said. After this the singing began. Water Monster finished the first set of songs. "Go ahead, now you help out!" Down Hogan was told. He put down a set of his songs. The Mallard Young Men were told: "Go ahead, put down a set of your songs," which they did. And (in) this (way) they were becoming his songs. Mud-hen Young Men put down some of their songs, Big Snipe also put down a set of his songs. A chance was also given to the small kind of snipe, and he also gave a set. A chance was also given to Curlew Young Men, (and) American Bittern Young Men, (and) Round-bill Crane Young Men, who also placed a set of their songs among the others. A chance was given the Snowy Egret Young Men, who also gave a set of their songs. And a chance to the *nahabił* Crane Young Men who also added their songs to the others. The (Speckled?) Crane People Young Men also put some of their songs among them. The *tó níłhęshii* Young Men also added some of their songs among them. The Grouse Young Men also contributed some. The Sandhill Crane People Young Men also contributed some of their songs with the others. All the flying ones (had a chance).

60. Next, here in the south, the people from a place called White Spot-under-water (were given a chance).[32] From a place called Mountain Pair Lies-at-water-center, from a place called Mountain Pairs Lie-about-at-water-center, to Toad Old Man (from these places), a chance was given: "Come on, add some of your songs (to the others)," he was told, which he did. To Green Frog Young Men "Go ahead!" was also said. Tadpole Young Men, from a place called White

[32]Mentioning of these "peoples" occurs again later on in the list of prayersticks. The place names are probably mythical.

Haliotis, also added some of their songs to the others. Tadpole Young Men, from a place called Smooth Surface Water, also put some of their songs among the others. Beaver Young Men from the "bridge" also added some to the others. To Otter Young Men from White Spot-under-water also the chance was given. They also put some with the others. To Water Turtle Young Men from White Spot-under-water also a chance was given. (Land) Turtle Young Men from White Spot-under-water also put some of their songs with the others. Waterdog Young Men from Water Circle also put some of their songs with the others. To Water Snake Young Men from the place called Wide Lake also a chance was given. And a chance given to Arrow Snake Young Men from the place called Body-of-water (Water Body) in-the-sky.

61. Dawn appeared. Toward the dawn the *yé'ii bicheii* (Talking-god) gave his call. A little closer he again gave his call. And from (a spot) a little closer again he gave his call, so three times he gave his call. Along the entrance he again gave his call, so that four times he had given his call. He entered followed by Calling-god. "You did not inform me of this, yet I came," he said. "Me also you have not informed, yet I came," said Calling-god. "Some of my songs shall be among them. I have difficulty in speech," said Talking-god. Calling-god repeated the same (and) finished singing some of his songs among them. One of those (small) Bluebirds came running up from somewhere (and) they also finished singing some (a set), placing themselves along the outside, one behind the other. Blue Swift Young Men also entered and finished some songs. Yellow Speckled Bird Young Men also entered (and) finished some songs. Cornbeetle Young Men also entered (and) finished some songs. There all (had finished).

62. Here that Old Man Water Monster finished its blessing (rite) song, they say. "Now then, you may depart! There is nothing more to be done. You may depart for your homes," he said. That was the end, they say. That Down Hogan (Man), mentioned before, alone stayed around there. Both of his grandmothers, too, were there.

13. The Non-sunlight-struck Girls of the Wide House

63. To these he spoke: "My Grandmothers, where is the place called Wide House?" he asked. "Stop! my Grandchild. You must not mention it. That is a place full of risk," she told him. "What is to be had there that you know of, my Grandchild?" she asked. "Well, I want to go to (those) upon whom (sunlight) never shines."[33] "Stop that, my Grandchild, that is a place full of danger, everything protects them," she told him. "Nevertheless I am going there (that is settled), my Grandmother," he told her. "We will see what the young men along Riverward Knoll will say (about that). First, hold your peace!" she told him. "As a matter of fact, I shall presently go back there. Upon my return we will see how it can be (done)," Riverward Knoll Woman told him.

64. The rainbow, as before, she threw under herself, and after she stepped on it, it snapped away with her as quick as one can wink, they say. Over there she sat (alighted) in the midst of those children of hers.[34] There the Whippoorwill happened to be their door guard. She gathered the pollen of the Riverward Knoll plant. She also gathered pollen of the mind medicine (plant). She also gathered pollen of yellow thistle. She also gathered spurge pollen, that same which is called "my thumb" (plant). Thus four (types of) pollen were gathered.

65. "Now let the young men come inside, I will speak to them (just) once," she said. "Say Phoebe Young Men, being familiar with the *ajiłee* rite, you will assist with your garment. Mockingbird, being familiar with the *ajiłee* rite, you will assist with your garment. You too, Canyon Wren will assist with your garment. You, Young Man Rock Wren, will assist with your garment and with your laughter too. You too, Young Man Woodpecker, will assist with your garment being familiar with the *ajiłee* rite. You too, Daredevil, will assist with your garment. While you will assist with your garment at the very top where he enters to those non-(sun)light-struck ones," was said to Big Butterfly. "As for

[33]Non-(sun)light struck ones is used in the translation.

[34]The poisonous weeds are called her children. These are mentioned in the following sentence.

you, Cornbeetle, you will assist there with your garment and with sounding your call," he was told. "So it is," it was said. They (all) agreed.

66. After that she stepped on that rainbow for her return and snapped back with it. She returned over there to her Grandchild and gave him this Riverward Knoll pollen, mind medicine pollen, yellow thistle pollen and spurge pollen, four (kinds of) pollen all told. "You have planned a journey to (one) not to be trifled with, my Grandchild," she told him. "When you enter to them over there, clothe yourself with the Big Butterfly (appearance). After flying over them four times in a circle, alight between them (where) the two are seated (and are) sewing a fabric. Now so it is, you see, my Grandchild. As for us, we are about to return to Riverward Knoll. Right there we will be living," she said. "As for what is taking place now, it will be called the meeting line for a short distance of the Waterway and the *ajiłee*," she said (where the myths of Waterway and *ajiłee* run parallel). "On this side (of the line) the Waterway will be stringing along," she said, "on the other (side) the *ajiłee* blessing (rite) line will (string) along," she said. "Now go on, my Grandchild, start off! We also will start back now. Sometime or other we may come upon each other again," she said.

67. Those two grandmothers of his started out to return. At once Say Phoebe came up. "Clothe yourself in my garment, my Grandchild," he said. People were numerous there. And so he was flying about nearby in it (garment), giving his call and alighting here and there. As for these people, in whose midst he had been, they said: "Wonder where Down Hogan went! Clearly his footprints lead just to this one place," they said. "That (bird) there alone is running around here simply giving its nice call, but would that be he?" they were saying. Again he clothed himself in the garment of that Mockingbird (and, coming) from the other side of a ridge he was talking and would alight here and there. While flying about it happened that around here a Canyon Wren was dancing up and down on a rock. That garment of his he threw towards him. In this he again traveled pretty far from there, when a Rock Wren, perched on a rock, was laughing. He, too, was dancing up and down.

68. In his (garment) he again traveled farther on from there, running on along the top of those rock ledges. No notice at all was taken of him, they say. And so those garments he would return to them (to birds) one after another. He was still going along when around there a Woodpecker again was standing, who again handed him his garment. "Here, my Grandchild, is my garment, get into it!" he said. And in this he ran along the trees standing in groves, pretending

repeatedly to peck at the trees here and there. He was still running along when around there a Daredevil again was walking about. "Here is my garment, my Grandchild," he said. From there simply running on the (sides) of trees he (gradually) approached them. Just a short distance away stood the Wide House. After a while he arrived below it, they say. Again he clothed himself in that Big Butterfly (garment). With the (four types of) pollen which his grandmothers had given him he rubbed the entire surface of his (wing) feathers, applying them to himself. With this he flew in. A transparent stone was there.[35]

69. About that time it was midday. The sun never shone on them at any time, they say, without ever reaching them. The light would travel along there, they say. Facing the rear part (of the room) the two sat there. With their fronts turned toward the rear part (of the room) and sewing a fabric the two happened to be seated there. After flying over them four times in a circle, he shook himself, causing the pollen which he had put on his wings to sprinkle on them. They noticed something along the side of their temples and, when his shadow began to move along at the place where the light shone, they followed him with their eyes. He alighted between them, they being seated with their backs toward each other. He spread out his wings under them (they looking down at him). The older one said: "Isn't that a beautiful (thing), my Older Sister! Let us sew such a pattern," she said. She called her younger sister "my Older Sister." "What are you saying, my Older Sister?" the younger said, "why, I am your younger sister," she said. "Catch it, we'll pattern according to it, my Older Sister," said the older one. "My Older Sister," she said to her younger sister, being attracted (by him).

70. "Stop that, my Older Sister, you never can tell what they (will do)! Stop! they tell us," she said. "But anyway, we will catch it, come what may, my Older Sister," said the older. "Even so, you have simply an ugly way of calling me a relative," she (the younger one) said. He would merely continue to spread his wings in their midst, while they looked on from both sides. After a while both were drawn on. From her position the older one wanted to put her hand over him, but he slipped through her fingers. The younger (tried) to put her hand over him but again he slipped through. From there he fooled them along to the place where (poles of a ladder) had been leaned up, the poles being of white bead shell and the four rungs of that same material. While the older one vainly tried to put her hand over him, and he continued to slip through her fingers, and the younger one doing likewise, he fooled them (to step) on one of the rungs after a while.

[35]This crystal probably served as a mirror or reflector.

71. From there he fooled them (to step) on the second white shell rung. Where the third white shell rung was, (on this) he again fooled them. (From there) he again fooled them on the fourth white shell rung. The older (girl) said: "To here (this far) permission had not been given us, (I know) my Older Sister," she said meaning her younger sister. "In vain I try not to want it, in vain it dissatisfies me," said the younger one. In vain he strove to lead them on, they say, by going towards them and back, and continually offering them a chance, but he (finally) fooled them from above down to the ground.[36]

72. Again he proceeded further on with them. At the center of a wide (corn)-field they could not be induced to go farther. Two squash (plants) stood side by side here, and it happened that another squash (plant) stood nearby. As (for a moment) they paid attention to themselves only, he clothed himself again in that garment of the Corn-beetle, and went into one of the yellow squash blossoms, which closed over him. With the sound *lo-o-o* he gave his call. Turning that way the two approached it from the east side, where they stood. "Around here it must have called, my Older Sister," she said. She spoke to her younger sister. "Listen, (how) beautifully it calls," she said. Again they approached it from the south side and stood there. "Whereabouts is it calling?" she said. Again the two approached and faced it from the west side. "Right about here it is calling. It surely calls beautifully," she said. From the north side again they approached it. "Whereabouts can it be calling? Is it at the root? Is it under its leaves?" she said.

73. Inside of that yellow blossom he arose in the form of man. He put his left arm around the older one, and his right arm around the younger, embracing both. "I said right along, that it is that way, my Older Sister," said the younger one, who now mentioned the relationship properly. "Now then, you have become mine for good," he said to them. The younger spoke: "It is a known fact, that so-called Earth People know everything. About this,[37] I suppose, time will go on (will pass) as you continue to act as our protector," she said to him. At once they plucked flowers, any and all that were beautiful. Whipping each other with them, they were thus creating affection for one another. After that, putting his arms around them, he started eastward with them toward La Plata Range. Showing their love for one another as they went along, they traveled quite a distance. He placed them in the lead and, telling them "let us go," the two started going ahead of him.

[36]Reference is, of course, to the Pueblo house. After fooling the girls out of their room to the rooftop, he flies back and forth there, then entices them to the ground level.

[37]She seems to refer to their breach of the village custom which kept them in seclusion.

14. Thunder Man

74. As soon as he lagged behind a little, he raised his left foot, and at that moment someone said "shd!" to him. With his foot still raised, he stood there and looked around in vain. He drew his right foot up to take a step, and again someone gave the same call. Again he looked around in vain. He again raised his left foot to step and again someone called "shd!" to him. Again he looked around in vain. His right foot again he raised to step and "shd!" again someone said to him. Suddenly he saw someone extending out from within the earth. "Come here, my Grandchild," he spoke. He proceeded to that spot, but found that the passageway in was (just) so narrow (in size). "How can one go down into so narrow an opening, my Granduncle?" he asked him. "Oh no, it is wide, my Grandchild." Saying this he blew into it (and lo!) the hole increased in size. And it happened that from it a ladder extended, having four crossbars one above the other.

75. Down in there he descended, which turned out to be Horned Toad Old Man's home. "A mighty one you have bothered, my Grandchild," he told him. "Do you possess any jewels?" he asked. "Yes, I own them," he replied. "Are there any white shell beads?" he asked. "There are some," he answered. "Is there any turquoise?" "There is some," he answered him. "Is there any abalone shell?" "There is," he told him. "Is there any jet?" "There is," he answered. "I see you have them all, my Grandchild," he said. "He is a person without mercy, my Grandchild, still I usually conquer him," he said to him. "As for me, those particular jewels shall be my offering in future days, that's settled," he said. "Here I happen to have the wherewith of conquering him (for good)," he said. He went to the rear of his hogan, brought out a dark flint and said: "When it has taken place four times, put this into

(your) mouth. Blow upward with it and say: 'Stay up!'"[38] "All right, my Granduncle, I can now start again (with this in my possession)," he said after he had received it from him.

76. From there he returned out and proceeded to follow in the direction which the two had taken. There was a (horizontal) ridge, small in size, over which the two had gone (and lo!) here they were sitting. It so happened that they had picked nice flowers and were playing with them. The older (sister) said: "Yuh! Where have you been (all this while)?" "I have been sitting right nearby," he told her. After that they did love-making again, tumbling about with each other (as they went along). At the white streak of water they arrived. Above them a cloud appeared which began to spread out just above their heads. Again the older one spoke: "Since it is a fact that, as the saying goes, the Earth People know (things), be sure to be doing it with all your might." Saying this she embraced him. "All right," he said to her.

77. Heavy raindrops splashed directly around them. Lightning struck the ground (and) shot up the dust on the east side. "Look out!" that Little Wind warned him. "Up above you are (and stay)," he said to it. "Look out! He is aiming at you again," that Little Wind said (to him). On the south side again it struck the ground, again it shot up the dust. Again he blew (at it). "Up above you are!" he said to it. "Look out he is trying (to hit) you again," said Little Wind. On the west side Lightning again struck, again it shot up the dust. "P-ah, up above you are!" he said to him and again blew (towards the sky). "Look out! He is trying for you again," said Little Wind. On the north side Lightning struck ground again and shot up the dust. "P-ah, up above you are!" he again said to him. That Little Wind again spoke out: "Look out! Into the top of your head (he is trying). Now put the dark flint into your mouth (and) blow (out) with it," he told him.

78. When there was another crash, a horizontal streak appeared way above (him). He blew out with that dark flint. The *yi-i-i* rumble sound died away. The low *yi-i-i* sound was heard, the noise died away returning to the south. The (low) *yi-i-i* was heard, the noise died away in the west. The (low) *yi-i-i* was heard, again the noise died away toward the north. That completed the set number. "It is true, you do know the power (of things)," the younger one said to him.

[38] Reference is to the custom of blowing out when there is a crash of thunder, and telling him to stay up in the skies (Sandoval).

15. Touching up of Prayersticks

79. Again they went farther on. Ahead of them people were running about, but what appeared to be humans running were only bluebirds. When they (the three) had winked just a little again, they saw them running about again in real human form. These they approached and faced. "Around here Earth People may not go about. From which place do you come," one of them asked. "What about you, where are you from?" he said to them. "To be sure, we are from Bluebird Mountain,"[39] he said. "Is there (any) turquoise?" he asked. "There is some," he answered. "Is there any white bead shell?" "There is some," he answered. "That shall be our offering in exchange for the information I shall give," he told him. What is called mind,[40] what is called thought, he gave him. "According to this you shall now be traveling," he told him. "When the offering of each one of these various people is made it shall be touched (with them),"[41] he said. "Thereby it will be recognized (by the receiving deity)." In accordance with this (instruction) the touching of prayersticks is done (at present). "All right," he said. "I understand how it is. Now we shall be going again."

[39]South of Santa Fe, New Mexico.

[40]Mind and thought to direct their travels is given to him for the people of the earth. And from the context it appears that the prayersticks are to be touched up with mind and thought, and thereby the divinity can recognize the offering. Does the person offering the gift express his mind and thought by touching up, or is mind and thought given the patient by this ceremony of touching up? The meaning is not clear.

[41]"Touching up" must be done by the patient. Dipping water with a plume the patient touches the prayerstick surface and says a prayer like "may I walk nicely" or any other he may choose. After this ceremony the usual ritual prayer is said to the prayer-stick by the singer and is repeated verbatim by the patient who holds the prayersticks (Sandoval).

16. Old Man Toad

80. They traveled on again in the direction of "him who wins them one after another" (a notorious gambler), when, for some reason or other, a stubby rainbow was stretched again over their path. "Wonder what it is," he was thinking as they were approaching that point. They approached within a short distance of it, when they found a cornfield where someone was hoeing (along) in a sitting position. He was hoeing with what is called a push-hoe, they say, (and) blowing (softly whistling) a song (tune) to himself. When they reached him he continued to hoe right along, without bothering about them, while they, too, did not speak to him. It just occurred to him about (the fellow with the hoe): "Isn't it strange! The Old man hoeing along there surely has long feet," he thought. "Yes, my Grandchild, I surely am that way. My feet are long for a fact," he answered him, he on that side (the frog) spoke.

81. To him (on this side) the thought again occurred: "How strange, the old man hoes along having legs that surely are very long," he thought. From that side again he spoke: "Yes, my Grandchild, I surely am that way. Having very long legs indeed I hoe along," he said. Again he thought of him: "How strange! The old man hoes along without having any buttocks," he thought. "That is right, my Grandchild, I am just that way, I go along hoeing for a fact, without having any buttocks," he said. Again it occurred to him: "How strange! Surely the old man hoes along having a very short spine," again he thought. "That is correct, my Grandchild, I surely am that way. I hoe along for a fact with just so short a spine," he said. Again he thought of him: "Clearly, the old man hoes along, his skin being just rough-like," he again thought. "So it is, my Grandchild, my skin is rough-like and (in that shape) I hoe along for a fact," he again said. Again he thought of him: "Clearly, the old man hoeing along has a head just so wide (quite wide) and eyes which are even with the surface," he again thought. "Yes that is it, my Grandchild, with a head so wide and eyes even with the (body) surface I hoe along, I do," he said to him.

82. Again he thought of him: "Clearly, the old man, with a chin bulging out, goes along hoeing," again he thought. "yes that is it, my Grandchild, with my chin bulging out I do go along hoeing," again he

said to him. Again he thought of him: "Clearly, the old man goes along hoeing, his mouth just so wide," his thought was again. "Yes that is so, my Grandchild, with a mouth so wide I do go along hoeing," he said to him. "Around here Earth People do not go about, my Grandchild," he said to him. "Even so, I want you to help me, for that purpose I am now here, my Granduncle," he told him. "In what manner shall I help you, my Grandchild?" he asked. "I am on my way to the (notorious) winner. This I want you to think over for me, my Granduncle," he told him.

83. In that case, "Have you any white shell?" he asked. "There is some, my Granduncle," he answered. "In that case is there any turquoise?" he asked. "There is some, my Granduncle," he answered. "In that case, is there any white-red abalone shell?" he asked. "There is that, my Granduncle," he told him. "Hand them over to me!" he said. "Do you have tobacco to prepare a smoke for me?" he asked. "I have some, my Granduncle," he answered. "In that case, do you also have tobacco to prepare smoke for me, my Granduncle?" he asked him. "There is some, my Grandchild," he said. "Do you have a tobacco pouch, my Grandchild?" he asked. "Do you also have your tobacco pouch, my Granduncle," he asked him. "I have it, my Grandchild," he answered. "Is the sun (figure) set upon it?" he asked. "Has yours also the figure of the sun on it, my Granduncle?" he asked him. "Is the moon's figure also on it, my Grandchild?" he asked. "So it surely is, my Granduncle," he told him. "Has yours also the figure of the moon on it, my Granduncle?" he asked. "So it has indeed, my Grandchild," he answered.

84. "Do you have the tobacco which is put into it, my Grandchild?" he asked. "That I have my Granduncle," he answered. "Do you also have what is put into it, my Granduncle?" he asked. "I have that, my Grandchild," he answered. "Do you have (something) to light it with my Grandchild?" he asked. "I have it my Granduncle," he answered. "Do you also have a lighter, my Granduncle?" he asked. "I have it, my Grandchild," he said. "Hand it over to me!" he said again. "Take out the bag, my Grandchild and lay it here," he said. Having taken it out he laid it down there. "You too, take out your bag, my Granduncle," he told him. And he taking it out laid it down. He picked them up, looked at them on the side where the sun figure was and laid them side by side. He turned them over on the other side where the moon (figures) were, looked at them (and) said: "Take out the pipe, my Grandchild." He did this. "You, too, take out (your) pipe, my Granduncle!" he told him. He produced it.

85. "What (kind of) pipe is it, my Grandchild?" he asked. "It is a turquoise pipe," he said. "What is the design on it, my Grandchild?"

he asked. "It is designed with white shell, of course, my Granduncle," he answered. "And yours, what is it (made of)?" he asked. "It is a turquoise pipe, my Grandchild," he answered. "The surface part, what is it?" he asked. "It is designed with white shell, of course, my Grandchild," he said. "What is it lighted with, my Grandchild?" he asked. Having produced a transparent stone he placed it on top of it (the pouch). "And you, what do you use for lighting it?" he asked. Producing a transparent stone (rock crystal) he placed this upon it. "Give it (here)!" he said.

86. He rose quickly, he stretched himself, he looked around. He, too, rose quickly, he stretched himself, he looked around. Having stepped toward him he placed his hand over his heart holding it for a time. Ha! he breathed. He stepped over to him (to the frog), laid his hand over his heart holding it there for a time. In the same manner as (the other) had done, he (too) breathed Ha! He patted him on the shoulders and said: "It is true, you are indeed my Grandchild!" The other also patted him on his shoulders and said: "It is true, you are indeed my Granduncle!" From this side he spoke first again: "Go ahead, my Granduncle, prepare a smoke for me!" he said. "Why don't you prepare one for me, my Grandchild?" he answered. From his earfolds the Little Wind said: "If you prepare it for him first, he will smoke nicely," he told him, "but if he prepares it first, something bad (poisonous) he (will) slip in (and) try you out with it," said Little Wind. "Let it be you, you prepare me a smoke, my Granduncle," he told him.

87. (So) at once he picked up the pipe mentioned. Taking the tobacco out of the pouch he put some into (the pipe), picked up the lighter mentioned and started a song. He held it up toward the Sun, they say; with that rock crystal he lit it, they say; smoke went up, they say; he took a draw of it, they say; so he did, they say; on the earth he blew with it, they say. He took another draw with which he again blew toward the earth; he took another draw and blew this toward the sky. What he had blown on the earth side he had done for vegetal life. What he had blown on the upper side he had done for (the purpose of) Male Rain, they say. That second puff on the earth side he had made for the purpose of bringing into being (all kinds of) vegetal pollen. And the last puff which he had blown on the upper side he had made (for the purpose) that dew and water iron ore might come into being (at all times).

88. "Draw four times on it and swallow (it) four times," he told him. He did as directed and, having taken four draws he swallowed (them). He gave it to him (to frog), after which he began to smoke it and finished smoking it entirely. He gave (the pipe) back to him again. "Ha!" he breathed, "now you prepare me a smoke, my Grandchild,"

he said. He picked up that turquoise pipe, took tobacco out of his pouch and filled (the pipe). He (then) picked up that rock crystal, he held it up toward the sun, held it to that tobacco (and) smoke went up. He took one puff of it which he blew on the earth. He took another draw, which he blew on the sky. Another puff he blew on the earth, and the next puff on the sky again.

89. The puff which he had blown the first time earthward was for the purpose of (securing) vegetal life. The next puff upward had been done for Male Rain. The next puff on the earth again he had blown that (various kinds of) vegetal pollen might come into being at all times. The last puff blown upward he had done that dew (and) water iron ore might always come into being.

90. So far this so happened. "What I spoke to you about the jewels, I said in order that these shall be my offering," he said. "They certainly shall be your offering, my Granduncle," he answered. "All right, my Grandchild," he said. "He certainly is not a common person, this so-called (notorious) winner (gambler)," he told him. "Simply going into his mouth (that sort of person) is called,"[42] he said. "Hoop-poling is (one) method I know of by which he wins from them," he said. "Seven dice is a known method by which he wins from them," he said. "Putting a (small) field rat into the ball[43] is (one of his methods) of winning from them," he said. "By the legs (racing) he wins from them, my Grandchild," he told him. "Even so, although these (facts) are as you say, this racing in particular (it is) for which I say this,"[44] he said. "Well, in that particular line he (most) frequently wins. Tell him you (will take) that, my Grandchild," he told him. "Then, of his winnings in women there are ten, of his own wives there are two, so that he has twelve wives," he told him. "When you have arrived there (at his home), you will see that he will nicely place his wives in a row," he said. "You too, must place your wives in line," he said. "But of this I will not inform you, my Grandchild," he told him. Well! I possess a way of getting information, he thought, so I don't care. "Now go ahead, my Grandchild, let us go!" he said.

[42]Like running into certain death.

[43]This is the shinny game *n'dilkal*. Here, however, not merely driving the ball over a goal line was meant. It appears rather that the ball had to be driven through a hole in a wall. Others speak of a hole in a board. By hiding a field rat in the ball he was able to make the goal every time.

[44]The forms "he said, asked" indicated that he is asking the Toad: "What about choosing a foot race with him?"

17. Wren Youths

91. So from there they started out,[45] when it happened that nearby, along the tips of the rocks, someone was walking about up there. Upon him again they came, and found that this was Canyon Wren Young Man. "In this neighborhood Earth People are not allowed. Whence do you come?" he asked. "It is simply the (notorious) winner to whom we are going, my Granduncle," he said. "Did you go (to see) Frog Old Man?" he said. "What is the name of the place there, my Grandchild?" he asked. "It is unknown, I do not know it," he answered. "I can inform you, my Grandchild," he said. "All right, my Granduncle, tell me then," he said. "Do you happen to have white (shell) bead with you?" he asked. "I do," he answered. "That must be my offering," he said. "Sure, my Granduncle, tell me (now)," he answered. "Cornfields-upon-which-one-gazes, that is the name of the place," he said.

92. They started out again. From there they went on again some distance, and so just a short distance remained (to be traveled), when along the rim of a rock someone again was walking about. They again came upon him. Now this happened to be Rock Wren Young Man. They approached him. But he laughed out loudly and out of his laughter (out of his mouth) he spoke: "In this neighborhood Earth People are not allowed," he said. "Oh, we are simply on our way to (notorious) winner," he replied. "It is well known to me how (notorious) winner stands," he said. "He certainly is a mighty one, my Grandchild. I can inform you," he told him. "All right, my Granduncle, come on then, inform me," he said to him. "Do you happen to have abalone shell, my Grandchild?" he asked. "There is some, my

[45] The Toad has not been mentioned by name in the preceding chapter. This is done in the following.

Granduncle," he replied. "All right, my Grandchild. You see, that must be my offering," he said.

93. "When you have come from here to him he will call you 'my friend' and say *'eng, eng'* to you, (then) he will rub his leg against yours," he said. "Directly he will smile towards these (two) women," he said. "Do not by any means smile at him, absolutely beware of doing this," he said to them. "Simply hang your heads down because of it," he told them. "Why do you say this, my Granduncle?" the man asked. "Should you smile (back) at him you would feel weak,[46] there should be no strength (life) in your limbs. Therefore it absolutely must not be (done)!" he said (to them). You see here he again continued: "Concerning his wives, you too, must smile at them. All of them will smile at you," he said. "There will be no life in his limbs, his strength will fail him," he said. "All right, we shall do this, my Granduncle. Now we can again continue on, my Granduncle, (feeling) assured," he told him. They then started on again.

[46]Should you see your wives smile at him, sex jealousy would cause you to weaken.

18. Spider Man

94. Here right nearby his house[47] came into view (and) he was living at a place called Braced-(under)-rock. They again passed along a place called Spider Mountain. Unexpectedly someone said "shd!" to them. They started on again when "shd!" was repeated. Again they started on when "shd!" again was repeated. Again they started on and again someone called "shd!" to them, four times (in all). Behind them, somewhat below them (at their feet), his eyes followed (the sound), when he noticed someone hanging out (of the ground). "Let us go. You too, go along and wait for me! Right (over) there you must wait for me," he said. He returned to that spot and there, far down, one was sitting. "Come in, my Grandchild," he told him. "Why is it, (why do you say this) my Granduncle? The opening is certainly very thin. How then can I get down into it?" he asked. "The place is big, my Grandchild," saying this he blew at (upon) it. He entered down in there (and) it turned out that this was Old Man Spider.

95. "Around here Earth People are not allowed. From where do you come (along), my Grandchild?" he asked. "I (am determined to) go to (notorious) winner, my Granduncle," he answered. "He is not a common person, my Grandchild. People usually go to him (and never return), my Grandchild," he said. "Hoop-poling is one means by which he wins them. Seven dice is another by which he wins," he said. "Ball is another with which he is wont to win, a hole of this (small) size being made through it (the wall) into which, when he hits the ball,[43] he thereby wins," he said. "His legs are another means of winning. By running a foot race with them (with people), he outruns and usually wins (over) them," he said. "Did you stop at that place called On-cornfields-one-gazes?" he asked. "There I did stop, my Granduncle," he answered. "What did Old Man Frog say to you?"

[47] His house, not his hogan.

he asked. "I know well enough what his[48] thought, what his sayings are," he said. "Go ahead then, tell me, my Granduncle," he said to him.

96. "Do you happen to have jet in your possession?" he asked. "There is some, my Granduncle," he answered. "All right," he said. He then told him that all Holy People upon whom he had come in the past would come together. "From the summit of *sisnaajiní* there will be a meeting of the Small Bird People, Bluebird People will come together," he told him. "From the summit of Mount Taylor Blue Swift People will meet," he said. "From the summit of the San Francisco Peaks Small Speckled Yellow Bird People will meet," he said. "From La Plata summit Cornbeetle People will meet," he said. "From the place called Water-bottom-white-spot the Water People will meet," he said. "From the place called White-tipped Mountain Thunder People will meet," he said. "From the place called Water-striped-(down) White Diving Crane People will meet," he said. "After these are gathered (there), you will go there from here, my Grandchild," he said. "Those (very) same (people) will conquer the person. Now go ahead, my Grandchild," he said.

97. He started to return (but found) his front obstructed with webs. That dark flint, which his granduncle had given him, he put into his mouth and with that he blew on them. Those webs dropped down (and) he returned out of there. A little after noon he had gone in there. And so it seems he had already pulled[49] it down (on the horizon). In reality he had spent the night down there. "My Grandchild, it surely cannot remain so! Restore my web for me," he pleaded. "When I have overtaken you and you are overburdened (with difficulties) I shall help you," he said to him. "All right, my Granduncle," he answered. He stepped towards that web, spat on it four times, rubbed it between his hands and it was restored. "It is true, you certainly are a holy person, my Grandchild, be on your way then," he said to him.

[48]As Spider does not await an answer but continues his speech, it is not quite clear to whom "his thought and sayings" refer. It is possible to refer this to the Toad as well as to the Gambler. The latter is probably meant, as the Spider is presumably an enemy of the Gambler.

[49]In popular belief the Spider has power to draw the sun down at will (Sandoval).

19. The Notorious Gambler

98. "What has happened (to me), am I not traveling with those women?"[50] With this thought in mind he started off. He simply[51] tracked those women along. Picking nice flowers and scattering them here and there on either side, they had traveled along, and soon he found them sitting there. He overtook them. The older one was holding a scarlet gilia, the younger held a bunch of (evening) primrose. "Yuh! whereabouts have you been?" she said. "Just any old place we spent the night." Saying this she whipped him with the scarlet gilia. Again the younger one spoke: "What were you doing that we should (be obliged to) spend the night any old place?" saying which she whipped him with the (evening) primrose. "It is only a short distance to the place now, let us go on!" he said to them. *Zo-zo-zo-zo* it sounded, the Wind began to run about.

99. It was found that he (the winner) used them in keeping watch there. At his (own) earfolds that Little Wind said: "Speak to them," he said. "Don't be doing that, Wind People, quiet down first,"[52] he said to them. Meanwhile, it seems, the Whippoorwill, who was the door guard over at Riverward Knoll, had glided over him and had shaken the scale (from his outspread wings) upon the (notorious) winner. When he had become sleepy, they entered his place. "Ha!" he exclaimed, "What has happened, my friend! This (entry of yours) escaped my notice!" he said. He stepped up to him. Saying *"eng, eng"* he rubbed his leg against his. (But) at once stepping up to (the winner) he rubbed his (own) leg against his.

[50] "How foolish of me to tarry so long! I should be traveling with those women!"

[51] That is, he had no difficulty in following their route.

[52] "First" gives the feeling of "for the time being, until I have reached my goal."

100. "Go ahead, which is it, my friend, hoop-poling perhaps?" he asked. "That? What can be done with it? That is not worthwhile!" he answered him. Nearby he again sat down a basket with seven dice. "That? What can be done with it! That isn't worthwhile!" again he answered him. Nearby again he laid down that shinny stick with the ball. "(Shall it be) this, perhaps?" he asked. "That? What can be done with it? That isn't worthwhile!" again he answered. "All right," he said. "Come on, we'll wager our wives," he said. On the north side his wives were lined up, his own (two) were on the side toward the south. "Choose any two of these you wish. I will wager them," he said. "Those two sitting in the center he loves (much)," said Little Wind at his earfolds. He selected these.

101. "You surely are a great one, my friend!" he said to him. "(But) come on! We'll run a foot race, shall we, my friend?" he asked. "Let all these people scattered about here be present, all of them without exception! Now one more thing I want to say to you," he told him. "All right, go ahead, speak out to me, my friend," he said. "Is it for (these) particular women on whose account one should entertain[53] hard feelings?" he said to him. "Go ahead my friend, whatever the point may be that you mean," he said. "Well, our bodies themselves, let that be the wager," he told him. "Let our lungs (heart), our heads be the wager," he said. "Be it so! That is the way one should talk!" he said. "Let us go to the race track!"

[53]Literally perhaps: "Should one's throat get dry after a long run?" (Sandoval).

20. The Foot Race

102. Much interested large groups had formed on both sides. On that side he stripped himself of his clothes, and he on this side also stripped himself. Those wives of his were lined up on the other side, while his two only were seated on this side. He looked along (the track). Not very far away there was a (horizontal) ridge. Beyond that again there was a ridge so that there were two (horizontal) ridges. Yonder still farther on there was a ridge and still farther on, almost out of eye-reach, there was a ridge, so that there were four (horizontal) ridges. At that point (in the distance) a mountain stood. It happened to be called the Floating Mountain.

103. Now Old Man Frog was going around there. Old Man Spider, too, was there, they say. "I shall do the marking," he said. "My grandchildren are running a foot race," he said. From yonder this way towards the people he drew the line, they say, that Old Man Spider did. While the people were busy there with one another, that Old Man Frog whispered into his grandchild's ear: "Be careful not to cross from your side to his, my Grandchild," he said. "Whatever you do, don't run on the side towards the north," he said. "Don't run ahead of him, but let him stay a little ahead of you and simply keep up his pace," he said. "When you reach that (nearest) ridge, do not check yourself any longer from there to this line. Now, go ahead!" he told him.

104. He put his foot on the line; this one also put his foot on the line. From there they dashed off and ran side by side.

105. No time at all had passed before that first ridge was passed. Over the other ridge farther on (they sped), then again over the third one. Way yonder they passed over the fourth ridge, still side by side. They encircled that mountain over there. In a very short time they both came out into view as black objects. This way along that ridge the first one came running, and behind him the other. And so the people that were gathered started in a mass from here and reached the top of that first ridge where they grouped. "Who is (the first runner)?" they were asking. "Perhaps (notorious) winner is running in the lead,"

they were saying, "perhaps Down Hogan is running in the lead, who knows?" they said.

106. Along the second ridge they were running side by side with (only) a short distance between them. In the meantime Old Man Toad had not urinated on the running side of his grandchild, but had urinated only on the running side of (notorious) winner, they say. Along the third ridge it happened that they were much nip and tuck. Even so, (notorious) winner was hanging somewhat in the lead. The wives of Down Hogan over there showed sorry looking faces, while his (own) wives showed much satisfaction. When they were drawing nigh, those people returned in mass beyond the goal line. From that ridge this way the two dashed along side by side toward the line. At that, he was still in the lead. When there were three steps more to be made, that (notorious) winner fell on one knee, (but) regained his speed with the other foot. Near the goal line, just when he (hero) had stepped next to the line, the other was again checked. He (hero) stepped across it, while this one had stepped on the center of the goal line.

107. What a shout went up from those partners of his! Even Toad Old Man was continuously dancing around. The boys of (notorious) winner all hung their heads. Nearby he was walking about puffing very hard, he on this side was doing likewise. At once he (gambler) picked up his axe, whatever it was that is called a movable axe. Although one should outrun him, they would strike themselves back with that (axe). "Go ahead, come on, while I am still hot!" he said. He (hero) quickly grabbed it (axe), they say, the other held his head toward him and said,"Come on." With (the axe) he struck the back of his head (and) chopped it up as he pleased.[54] And it seems that Hummingbird had already run away with the big bead which used to hang around his neck, and which gave a sound whenever he ran his races.

108. With this he flew four times in a circle above the people, then flew to a patch of beeweed with it. Out of the interior of his (the gambler's) head a flock of butterflies flew up. Where this (flock) ended a white butterfly came out. Those butterflies had gone out among the nice flowers. Following them, with little life left in his limbs, went that white butterfly. From his earfolds that Little Wind told him: "Yonder is the one from whom you have won his legs, the former (notorious) winner. Into the form of a white butterfly he has gone," he said. Up to this time he did not bother those wives of (the gambler), while (now) he started to return with his (own) wives. Then all the people departed.

[54]The account does not explain why the axe did not rebound.

21. Thunder People

109. From there they started off again, and arrived on top of what is called White Mountain, (where) Thunder People happened to live. These owned zigzag lightning. "Around here Earth People are not allowed. From where do you come?" one asked. "You see, I want you to tell me something, for that purpose I am here, my Granduncle," he answered. "All right, my Grandchild, I shall (or can) certainly tell you something," he said. "Go ahead then, tell your name!" he told him. "Down Hogan they call me, of course, my Granduncle," he answered. "You shall make it according to this, my voice part. By that you shall be (able to) go on (and live). In days to come, by this you shall be enabled to live on," he told him. "As for any kind of tree which I strike, of that you shall make it,"[55] he told him. "Is there any jet?" he asked. "There is," he answered. "Have you any turquoise in your possession?" he asked. "There is some," he answered. "Do you own abalone shell?" he asked. "There is some," he answered. "Do you own white bead?" he asked. "There is some," he answered. "If in days to come you are to make an offering in place of a so-called Earth Person, let it be two of the jet kind," he said. "If the ceremony be held over a man, five jewels must be my offering," he said. "If it be a woman patient all of these jewels, of the white bead kind two, making five with these, must be my offering," he said. "Then, also, (for) my own upright you shall break (limbs) from four sides of that same (tree)," he said. "And in its surroundings you shall collect plants sunwise, and when the collecting has been done four times this will make the full number," he said.

110. "Here, to the side of the north, don't bring your tracks together.[56] Certain evil things which (may be) bothering one (usually) run out through there," he said. "Then (also) the limb of that same

[55]This reference to "making it" seems to apply to the groaning stick or bull-roarer, for which lightning-struck wood and pitch is used. While this would be sufficient to produce the "Thunder's voice," the groaning or "thundering" stick is not a specialty of this ceremony. As *álíil* or specialty of the Waterway ceremonial, a sort of a megaphone is mentioned. As far as I can learn this is a short, flute-shaped horn, the mouthpiece of which fits well over the lips. A loud sound can be produced. This *chooghǫ́ǫ́'* was known as the *álíil* of *tóee* which was featured at public corral dances as the specialty of singers of this rite. The informant does not mention this part of the pouch.

[56]The sunwise circle should be left open at the north terminal.

(tree) which extends toward the east shall be the poker," he said. "The limb of the same, extending to the south, that too shall be the poker," he said. "The limb of that same, extending to the west, this too shall be the poker," he said. "The limb of that same, extending to the north, that too shall be the poker," he said. "Then too, the bark, which is torn from that same (tree), shall also be (used)," he said. "And, concerning my upright, some of the same (tree) which I have charred, shall also be used for it," he said. "And all kinds of wood without exception shall serve you as an igniter," he said. At this point, finally, he spoke to him: "What shall we say (so) that it can become our igniter?" he asked. Here a song was sung for him.

111. Toward it has now taken his seat, now facing it, Dark Thunder has taken his seat,
When zigzag lightning goes away from it back and forth, from where it (usually) goes back (and forth),[57] *he is making trees in(to) white splinters one after another,*
Now causing darkness by it, now throwing flashes from him (in succession), with water dripping from it, as he makes one after another, he now sits facing it.

112. Facing it, Blue Thunder has now taken his seat,
When straight lightning goes back and forth away from him, from where it usually goes back, he causes white water sprays one after another.
Now causing darkness by it, with straight lightning going back and forth from him, with water dripping from it, he now takes his seat facing it.
E-ya-he yi-a-ni-yo.

113. This particular (song) has been given to us (for) the fire drill. "But how shall I name you when I make your offering?" he asked him. "'The Sounding-one-on-the-cloud-tip, Dark Thunder, Young Man Chief, your sacrifice I have made' you will say to me," he told him. "'Sounding-one-on-the-cloud-tip, Blue Thunder, Maiden Chief, I have made your sacrifice' you will say to me," he said. "'Sounding-one-on-the-cloud-tip, Yellow Thunder, Young Man Chief, your sacrifice I have made' you will say to me," he said. "'Sounding-one-on-the-cloud-tip, White Thunder, Maiden Chief, I have made your sacrifice' you will say to me," he said.[58] With this he had been told all.

[57]At the opposite end of lightning, its point or head, as lightning is always provided with an arrowhead.

[58]The respective stanzas for Yellow and White Thunder have evidently been omitted in the above song.

22. Pollen Shaken from Birds

114. They then started on again and arrived up at the summit of *sisnaajiní* Mountain. Here Small Bird People had their homes. "Around here Earth People are not allowed," one of them said. "There is something that you can tell me, therefore I came here, my Granduncle," he said. "Do you happen to have an unwounded buckskin?" he asked. "There is one," he answered. "Does it happen to be one on which the head can be recognized?" he asked. "You certainly can recognize it on this one," he replied. "Is there a turquoise tied at the top on the head end?" he asked. "There is that. It is just that way," he answered. "That then must be my offering. In exchange for it I can inform you," he told him.

115. "Going about as you do, my Granduncle, what means have you of knowing things?" he asked.[59] "It is true that I go about thinking nicely, my Grandchild," he replied. "You see, when you shake pollen from me, you must use it in decorating this thing you call the 'pouch'," he told him. "Then, too, this turquoise, after putting it into my mouth with pollen, shall be placed in your mouths while you recite the prayers," he said. "Concerning my earwax, which you gather too, you must practice listening with it," he said. "That is the thing I really meant, my Granduncle," he said to him. "That same *sisnaajiní* you shall be using in days to come," he said.[60] Here it slipped my memory who it was that said this.

[59] His earwax, because by "listening in," the Bluebird seems to know things. Its earwax is therefore used for this purpose, as explained farther on.

[60] His slip of memory, of which the informant speaks in the next sentence, leaves this passage unexplained.

116. From there they then departed towards Mount Taylor. They reached the summit of Mount Taylor. People somewhat bluish in appearance went about, and these happened to be the Blue Swift People. "Whence do you come? Around here Earth People are not allowed," one of them said. "There is a reason, my Granduncle, which is that you can tell me a certain thing," he answered. "Do you happen to have turquoise with you?" he asked. "There is some, my Granduncle," he answered. "That must be my own offering. In exchange for that I can tell you (what you desire)," he said. "Did you perhaps stop at White Mountain?" he asked. "We did, we came there and stopped," he answered. "Did you see the Thunder People?" he asked. "The most important thing he did not make known to you, my Grandchild," he told him. "All right, my Granduncle, come on then, let me know what it is," he said.

117. "The very upright which he has dedicated to himself, you must employ to make (ceremonial) uprights," he explained. "He certainly did not tell me that, my Granduncle," he told him. "This, you must know, is called Mount Taylor, my Grandchild. Here is the place, you must know, called the 'sky-hole'," he told him. "I see, so it is, my Granduncle," he said. "As future days go by, the pouch shall be made from here only. From here, too, the talking prayersticks alone can be made," he told him. "All right, my Granduncle, that was the purpose for which I came," he said.

23. At the Home of Water Monster

118. From there again they started on, but nothing in particular happened to them (until) they reached the place called White-spot Water-bottom. Here they came to the entrance and stood. The so-called reflected sunrays happened to be the (pair of) door guards. Here they entered (and saw) that Water Monster lay in the rear part of the room. "Whence do you come? Around here Earth People are not allowed," he said. "You see, I want you to tell me a certain thing, that explains my coming, my Granduncle," he told him. "All right," he said. They say that in the direction to the east (a body) of dark water extends. He picked up one of those stubby rainbows that were there. With this he moved that body of dark water, then raised it, as this water happened to be really a curtain.

119. He looked upon it and saw a large number of water horses. "What do you think this is, my Grandchild?" he asked him. From his earfolds that Little Wind (prompted): "With that he is testing you! Tell him water horse! If you do not guess correctly, you shall not leave the place, therefore he asks," he whispered to him. "Why, that is a water horse, my Granduncle," he answered. "That is it exactly, my Grandchild," he said. "Over there what is that?" he asked, referring to a pair on the east side, lying side by side with heads reversed. Again Little Wind whispered from his earfolds: "You see that is a pair of zigzag lightning lying with heads reversed, tell him." "Why that, my Granduncle, is a pair of zigzag lightning lying with heads reversed," he answered. "That is it exactly, my Grandchild," he said.

120. Again he stepped over to the south side, where there was another body of blue water. He repeated the same as he had done previously, he raised it again with (the rainbow). He looked inside again and saw many water horses, blue in color, spread out there. "What do you think this is, my Grandchild?" he asked. Again that

Little Wind prompted him from his earfolds: "Why, that is a water horse, my Granduncle," he answered. "That is it exactly, my Grandchild," he said. "Above them, what is that pair lying side by side with heads reversed?" he asked him. Again the one in his earfold whispered: "Tell him that is a pair of straight lightning lying with heads reversed." "Why, that is a pair of straight lightning lying with heads reversed, my Granduncle," he answered him. "That is it exactly, my Grandchild," he said.

121. From there he stepped again to the west side where a body of yellow water extended out. This he again moved with the same thing with which he had moved the others, and again raised it up with it. Again yellow water horses were there in large numbers. "What do you think this is, my Grandchild?" he asked him. The one in his earfolds, Little Wind, again said: "Tell him, 'Why, that is a water horse!'" he whispered. "My Granduncle, why, that is a water horse," he answered him. "That is it exactly, my Grandchild," he said. "The pair lying over them with heads reversed, what do you think that is?" he asked. From his earfolds again he prompted: "You see, a pair of sunrays heads reversed lies there, tell him," he whispered. "You see, a pair of sunrays heads reversed lies there, my Granduncle," he answered him. "That is it exactly, my Grandchild," he said.

122. Directly he again stepped over to the north side, where a body of white water extended. This he again moved with the same thing used previously and with it he raised it up. He also went there and stood, and there water horses, white in color and in large numbers were to be seen. "What, think you, is this, my Grandchild?" he asked. "Water horse, tell him," Little Wind whispered to him. "That is a water horse, my Granduncle," he told him. "That is it exactly, my Grandchild," he said. "That pair lying over them with heads reversed, what do you think that is?" he asked. "That is rainbow, tell him," Little Wind whispered. "Why, that is rainbow, my Granduncle," he answered. "That is it exactly, my Grandchild," he said.

123. In the east where he had first raised it, water horses black in color were floating about. Where he had raised it in the south, in the blue water, blue water horses were floating about. Under the west side where yellow water extended out, yellow water horses were floating about. Under the north side where white water extended, white water horses were floating about. "This east side door guard, what do you think it is, my Grandchild?" he asked. From his earfold Little Wind said: "Tell him that is a dark water pot which contains collected water inside, tell him," he whispered. "Why, that is a dark water pot which, with collected water inside, is its door guard," he answered. "So it is exactly, my Grandchild," he said.

124. "On the south side what do you think is its door guard, my Grandchild?" he asked. From his earfold he whispered to him: "You see, a blue water pot with spring water inside is door guard (there)," he said.[61] "So it is exactly, my Grandchild," he said. Referring to those in the west, "What do you think this is, my Grandchild?" he asked him. "Tell him, a yellow water pot, with male rain inside, is the pair of door guards," he whispered to him. "You see, my Granduncle, a yellow water pot with male rain inside is the pair of door guards," he answered. "So it is for a fact, my Grandchild, he said. "As for the north side, what door guard is it do you think?" he asked. "You see a pair of white water pots with female rain inside are door guards," he answered. "So it is in fact, my Grandchild," he said. "It is true, you are one of the Holy People, my Grandchild," he said.

125. "Even so, there is something more that I desire, tell me this (as we) proceed," he told him. "Over there I was not present, (I missed) part of it, my Granduncle," he said. "Which part do you mean, my Grandchild?" he asked. "You had finished the one night singing[21] when I arrived, at the time, my Granduncle," he answered. "It is true, so it did happen there, my Grandchild," he said. "On that account I should like to know the entire performance from the beginning on, my Granduncle," he said to him. "All right, my Grandchild," he said. "Do you happen to own jet?" he asked. "There is some," he answered. "Do you happen to own turquoise?" he asked. "There is some," he answered. "Do you happen to own abalone shell?" he asked. "There is some," he answered. "Do you happen to own white bead (shell)?" he asked him. "There is some," he answered. "Do you happen to own white and red abalone?" he asked. "There is some," he answered. "These are the things you must know, which will be the offering to me," he said. "All right, my Granduncle, for that purpose I mentioned the matter," he told him.

[61] "Water's Child" as the Navajo reads, denotes flowing or water from springs. "Collected Water" is water collected in pools, natural lakes, rock cavities, and the like. Opinions differ on this interpretation (Sandoval). It will be noted that both waters have a prayerstick assigned to them. Elsewhere too, they are treated much like other supernaturals, one being male and the other female.

24. Prayerstick Types of the Waterway Ceremony

126. "You should know, then, that there is a something with which my smoke must be prepared," he said. Now by this he referred to his prayerstick, they say. The prayerstick, then, of Water Monster is black, (and) with two names it is addressed. "Mountain Tobacco, Water Tobacco, these you shall place inside of it for me," he said. "With transparent stone (crystal) you shall light it for me, after (some) violet[62] has been rubbed on it. In that way I shall be pleased with it," he said. "The next prayerstick you must make blue in color for me," he said. "Mountain Tobacco, Water Tobacco you will put inside of it for me, then light it for me with transparent rock, and rub the surface (of the prayerstick) with violet. Then it will be pleasing to me," he said.

127. "Now, as for the insertions in these prayersticks, they are exactly identical for each prayerstick, their openings are stoppered with flag pollen.

128. "The prayerstick of the east side Water Horse is black. That of the south side Blue Water Horse is a blue prayerstick. That of the west side Yellow Water Horse is a yellow prayerstick. The north side White Water Horse has a white prayerstick. That completes this set.

129. "Next to these is the prayerstick of Rainboy, a black one. Raingirl's prayerstick is blue. Flash Lightning's[63] prayerstick is blue. Rainbow's prayerstick is blue on its lower half, red on its upper half. This completes this set.

[62]After the stick is cut the required length, its surface is roughened with a stone, then it is rubbed with dodgeweed, violet, or other plants for sizing. Violet is required for Water Monster's prayerstick. The following sentence implies that this same plant is used in sizing all prayersticks required in this chant.

[63]The flashes of lightning in summer nights which are not accompanied by peals of thunder (Sandoval).

130. "Black Thunder's prayerstick is black, Blue Thunder's is blue, that of Yellow Thunder yellow, that of White Thunder white. That completes this set. The prayerstick of Dark Cloud is black, that of Blue Cloud blue, that of Collected (Rain) Water is dark, that of Spring Water blue, which completes this set of prayersticks.

131. "The prayerstick of Male Rattlesnake is black, that of Female Rattlesnake is white, that of Male Arrowsnake is black, the prayerstick of Female Arrowsnake is blue.

132. "The prayerstick of Male Mallard is black, of the female blue. The prayerstick of Male Mud-hen is black, that of the female blue, which completes this set.

133. "The prayerstick of (the large) Male Jack Snipe is white, that of the female gray. By mixing colors (black and white) it becomes gray. The prayerstick of the small kind of Male Jack Snipe is white, that of the female again gray, which also completes this set.

134. "The prayerstick of the Male Twigbill (Crane) is yellow, that of the female again gray. The prayerstick of the (American) Male Bittern is blue, that of the female also blue, the difference being only in the mention of their names.

135. "The prayerstick of the (brown) Male Roundbill Crane is white, that of the female white, the difference being in calling them by their names. The prayerstick of the Male Snowy Egret is white, that of the female white. Only, they are called by different names.[64]

136. "The prayerstick of the *nahabił* (Crane) is white, that of the female white, only that they are named differently. The prayerstick of the (Speckled) Male Crane is blue, that of the female yellow.

136. "The prayerstick of the Male Toad is black, that of the female blue. The prayerstick of the Male Green Frog is blue, that of its female blue, with only a difference in naming them.

138. "The prayerstick of the Minnow is black, that of the female blue. The prayerstick of Tadpole is black, that of its female blue.

139. "The lower coat of paint on the prayerstick of Otter is yellow, the upper coat is of black spots. That of its female is likewise, the lower coat is again yellow, the upper again of black spots. The prayerstick of Beaver is a mixture resulting in a grayish color, with yellow spots for the upper coat (of paint). That of the female is identical.

140. "The prayerstick of the Water Turtle is blue, that of its female is also blue, they are just called by different names. The prayerstick of the Male Box Turtle is black, that of the female is likewise black, again only with the difference in naming them.

[64]The text does not continue the division of sticks into sets of four, but I have divided them so in the following, wherever possible.

141. "The prayerstick of the Male Waterdog is white, speckled in black, that of its female is gray, speckled in white. The prayerstick of Water Snake is black, that of its female blue. This is this set.

142. "From there on, the Horned Toad's prayerstick is black. For the upper coat of the male one, arrowheads are drawn upon it in white, butts and tips being reversed side by side. The prayerstick of the female is white with an upper coat of arrowpoints in black, tips and butts reversed.

143. "The Spider's prayerstick is black, that of its female gray. The prayerstick of Canyon Wren is gray, that of its female gray, with a difference again in naming them. The prayerstick of Rock Wren is blue, spotted red here and there on the surface. That of its female is also blue and again spotted red here and there on its surface, the difference being in the naming.

144. "The prayerstick of the Male White Butterfly is white, speckled with black, blue, yellow, and red (spots). That of its female is white and speckled again with all colors, the difference being only in the naming of them.

145. "Although these are strung along from (the first to here) in this manner, every last one of them has a talking prayerstick extending up behind them,[65] every last one glittering." Up to here he counted them out for him, they say. "That is the thing (I wanted), my Granduncle. In the future we (now) can live on by this," he said to him. "That is all, my Granduncle, to there. This, you see, I am saying. Although I told this much, the larger part is (still) missing. I was not told the whole of (this myth)."

[65]"Extending up behind them" has reference to the manner of depositing the sticks after the ceremony. The pair, male and female prayerstick, is laid down flat, while the talking prayersticks, tied together, are stuck into the ground just behind them (Sandoval).

25. What the Waterway Accomplishes

146. You see, as it sometimes happens, if a person be drowned (and rescued), this is a case where (Water) attaches a line to him.[66] Then, too, Thunder, on his part, (may) hold a person (responsible). Concerning Corn, too, (this is a case) if one derives injury from it. Or, if one should eat some kind of flag, he could be held by it. Inhaling (some) flag pollen, and thereby losing one's voice, might keep him held (responsible). These are cases in point. If one should use wood shattered by Lightning in preparing food, he could be held for that. Or, if one should eat sheep which were struck (by Lightning), he might hold one responsible to him. Or if one should eat horses so struck, or cattle so struck, if one should eat them he could hold a person responsible. Or if a person ate of a Lightning-struck cornfield, he could be held responsible. Or, if one should prepare food with wood of trees uprooted in the path of a strong wind, he could be held responsible for it.

147. So you see, if it be any of these instances mentioned, the thing may be remedied by it (this Waterway rite). Not that all of these causes will always help along, sometimes only a single one may cause it. (But) if the misfortune be caused along this line, one's dreams will usually tell a person (that) Water Monster is the cause. He fancies that he fell into the water (bottom). (Or) that Water Horse is the cause, (since) he fancies that he is drowning. Therefore, when his offering is to be made, the prayerstick of Water Monster is cut. On the side of the Water Horse it is done likewise, also if the Rainboy's be required, these (and other) prayersticks are cut as occasion demands. The prayersticks cut, jewels are set aside in sets of three. There is no set rule for this, as long as three kinds are put together.

[66]That is, the person is held responsible to Water, Lightning, Wind, etc., until the offense is righted by the ceremony (Sandoval).

26. How Prayersticks are Fixed Up

148. Directly one again puts down specular iron ore, or something else if one has it, then blue pollen, (and) flag pollen. Then of the small birds one puts down three feathers; any will do, such as those of the Bluebird or Wild Canary. Of these one of the wing feathers on each side is plucked out, and one of its tail feathers. This is called "as the flying is done." Next, one puts down a white down feather, next a turkey plume, next a turkey's broom (his beard), then some cotton twine. After that the shake-off (so-called "pollen"), Bluebird's shake-off, Corn Beetle's shake-off. Then finally, one touches those prayer-sticks twice, a tail feather, which has been plucked from a live Bluebird, one uses to touch them. Those down feathers, previously mentioned, are all carried twice along their surface.[41] Up to this point all is ready.

149. He (the singer) then picks up the pollen bag and, taking one stick at a time, he sprinkles the full length of it, saying: "From now on may you nicely do restoring. May you do restoring this very day." At once he applies it to the person for whom the ceremony is held, from his soles up to the top of his head. Some he puts into his mouth, some he sprinkles out,[67] and this is done that he may continue to walk on it. Then he (the singer) puts the prayerstick into his hand. The one first in rank one places at the bottom. After which, placing them one on top of the other, that last (prayerstick) comes uppermost.[68] Then there, facing the (patient), he sits down and speaks:

[67] Usually in front of the patient (Sandoval).

[68] First and last of any set or sets of prayersticks chosen by the patient. While a certain order has been observed in the following prayers, only such as have been chosen by the patient are recited. The informant was merely desirous of pointing out the invocations corresponding to the prayersticks listed above.

150. Water Monster of the Water-bottom White-spot,
Young Man Chief, I have made your sacrifice,
I have prepared your smoke.
This very day your power,[69] *which you may exert over him, you will remove from him!*
You have removed your power from him!
You shall carry it far away from him! You have carried it far away from him! Far away you will return with it! Far away you have returned with it!
May he nicely recover this very day! May the pains in him nicely cool off this very day!
May sickness nicely move away from him! May he nicely walk about!
May he go about with his body thoroughly cooled!
May he go about with his body thoroughly lightened!
May he go about full of energy! May he go about with no sickness on him! May he go about immune to sickness!
With his front in nice shape, may he go about! With his back[70] *in nice shape, may he go about!*
With all below[71] *him in good (nice) shape, may he go about! With all above him in nice shape, may he go about! With all his surroundings in nice shape, may he go about! With his speech always pleasant, may he go about!*
As one who is Long-life Happiness One may he go about!
Pleasant it has become again (four times).

At the Water-bottom White-spot, in the section of dark water, Water Horse, Young Man Chief,

[69]Power, charm, spell or magic convey the meaning of *álíil* here.

[70]In the prayer to the female prayerstick, these two lines are exchanged "with his back in nice shape" being recited before "with his front in nice shape." The informant stated that, even with a female patient he always makes the invocations to the male divinity first, which order is reversed by some singers. Alternations, as noted here, are very common practice in prayer and song to female divinities. Finally the informant has given the text of the prayer as recited for the patient. Actually the prayer is repeated word for word by the patient and throughout the prayer the I-form must be used, for instance, "You will remove your power from me which you are exerting over me," or, "with my front, back, etc. in good shape, I shall walk about." This praying by the patient is sufficiently indicated above, where the text states that the prayersticks are placed into his hands and that the singer faces the patient, both being seated.

[71]Where more than one prayerstick is chosen, this portion of the prayer is added at the close of the last prayer, and "pleasant it has become again" is repeated four times, otherwise only twice after each prayerstick prayer.

I have made your sacrifice, I have prepared your smoke.
(Therefore).... Water Horse at the Water-bottom White-spot, in the sections of blue water, Maiden Chief....
Water Horse at the Water-bottom White-spot, in the section of yellow water, Young Man Chief....
Water Horse at the Water-bottom White-spot, in the section of white water, Maiden Chief, I have made your sacrifice.

Rainboy above the skies, in a house of clouds, Young Man Chief, I have made your sacrifice, prepared your smoke....
Raingirl above the skies, in a house of water, Maiden Chief....

Flash Lightning above the skies, Young Man Chief, Flash Lightning above the skies, Maiden Chief.... Rainbow above the skies, Young Man, Chief.... Rainbow above the skies, Maiden Chief....

Dark Thunder who sounds along the cloud tip, Young Man Chief, and, Blue Thunder who sounds along the cloud tip, Maiden Chief.... Yellow Thunder who sounds along the cloud tip, Young Man Chief.... White Thunder, who sounds along the cloud tip, Maiden Chief.... sacrifice....

Dark Cloud, Young Man Chief, and Blue Cloud, Maiden Chief.... Collected (Rain) Water, Young Man Chief, and Water's Child, Maiden Chief....

Grayish Body (rattlesnake), in the hogan at the earth's center, Young Man Chief, and Grayish Body in the hogan at earth's center, Maiden Chief....

Sky Arrow (flying snake), at the sky place by name, Young Man Chief, and Sky Arrow in sky place by name, Maiden Chief....

Dark Mallard at Water-bottom White-spot, who sounds along the water surface, Young Man Chief, and Blue Mallard Maiden Chief.... Mud-hen at the Water-bottom White-spot, Young Man Chief, and Mud-hen Maiden Chief....

Jack Snipe, who walks along the water edge at Water-bottom White-spot, Young Man Chief and Maiden Chief.... Plover at the Water-bottom White-spot, Young Man and Maiden Chief....

Twigbill Crane (curlew?), who walks along the water edge at Water-bottom White-spot, Young Man and Maiden Chief.... Bittern, who walks on the water at Water-bottom White-spot, Young Man and Maiden Chief....

Roundbill Crane at the Water-bottom White-spot, Young Man and Maiden Chief.... Snowy Egret at Water-bottom White-spot, Young Man and Maiden Chief.... Nahabił Crane at Water-bottom White-spot, Young Man and Maiden Chief.... (Speckled) Crane at Water-bottom White-spot, Young Man and Maiden Chief....

Who-sits-on-dark-water (toad) at the two buttes in the center of the water, at the sections of dark water, Young Man, and Who-sits-on-blue-water-scum at the two buttes in the center of the water, at the sections of blue water, Maiden Chief....

Greenfrog, in the hogan of dark water, in the sections of dark water, Young Man Chief, and Greenfrog, in the hogan of blue water, in the sections of blue water, Maiden Chief....

Minnow at the Water-bottom White-spot, Young Man and Maiden Chief.... Tadpole at Water-bottom White-spot, Young Man and Maiden Chief....

Otter at the bridge, Young Man and Maiden Chief.... Beaver at the bridge, Young Man and Maiden Chief....

Water Turtle at Water-bottom White-spot, Young Man and Maiden Chief.... I have made your sacrifice.... Box Turtle at Water-bottom White-spot, Young Man and Maiden Chief.... Waterdog at Water Circle, slow moves at the water bottom, Young Man and Maiden Chief....

Water Snake of the Wide Lake, Young Man and Maiden Chief....

Horned Toad in the hogan at the center of the earth, at the sections of the earth, who lies on an earth wart (mud ball), Young Man and Maiden Chief....

Dark Weaver in the hogan at the center of the earth, whose hogan is (made) of the earth, at the sections of the earth, Young Man Chief, and Blue Weaver.... Maiden Chief....

Canyon Wren, whose hogan is of dark rock at the sections of dark rock, Young Man and Maiden Chief.... Rock Wren, whose hogan is of sparkling rock, Young Man and Maiden Chief....

White Butterfly in the valleys, Young Man and Maiden Chief....

27. Talking Prayersticks

151. The talking prayersticks are simply stuck into the ground behind them, no prayer is spoken for them. Reed alone is used in making all of them, without exception. For the talking prayersticks two are used, blue willow and, if there be none of this, red (bark) willow is used. The talking prayersticks are laid side by side, the male on the left, the female on the right side. The male one is black with a blue face (on which) eyes and a mouth are (painted). Across the forehead a white stripe is drawn, a blue one across its chin, and the top of its head is blue. The female is blue with a blue face like its body, eyes and mouth are (provided). A white stripe is drawn across its forehead, a yellow one across its chin. The top of its head is black. Under them a white (down) plume is placed, on top of this a turkey (down) plume. After that four (spiral) turns are wound around them with cotton twine, the line ending at the upper end.

152. Each one (of the prayersticks) is the length of a three fingers' width measure, excepting only the talking prayersticks (which are) a trifle longer and are tapered at the end to be stuck into the ground. Then only this prayerstick of the Toad is rubbed with frog corn (plant), while all the rest are rubbed with violet.

28. Depositing Places

153. At the depositing places each (of the prayersticks) is deposited only in the ordinary sunwise fashion. In this same way only, one after the other is deposited. These prayersticks of Water Monster, and that of Water Horse, are usually deposited toward some dry lake. The prayersticks of Rainboy, Raingirl, Flash Lightning, Rainbow are deposited at a spring. Those of Rain (Sky-) Water, of Spring (Earth-) Water, of male rain and female rain, if there be no flowing spring, they are deposited simply at a moist place. Thunder's particular prayersticks are deposited right at a lightning-struck spot. Below each one a bunch of dodgeweed is placed. Water Snake's prayersticks lie in position under greasewood. The Arrow (or flying) Snake's prayersticks lie at the water edge. If this cannot be done, they lie toward a willow. The prayersticks of the flying[72] beings have dry lakes for depositing places, without exception. As for the Toad's prayerstick, this is placed at points where the springs spread out. If that cannot be done, a moist place is selected. (Prayersticks for) Minnows and Tadpoles are placed in soil which has collected in the hollow of rocks or, if that cannot be done, in some dry lake.

154. As for lakes containing water into which quadrupeds go and come, such a place should not be used, since having them trampled upon and broken would be dangerous, for the reason that both the person for whom the ceremony was held, and the person performing it, could be held responsible. Therefore, only lakes without water (should be chosen). The prayersticks of Otter, Beaver, Water and Box Turtles are placed in ordinary dry lakes, those of the Waterdog and Water Snake at bodies of water to which there is no (easy) approach. If that cannot be done they are placed at any dry lake. The prayerstick of Horned Toad is placed next to an "earth wart."[73] That of Spider in its own home, or if that cannot be done, simply at any cobweb. Those of all Canyon Wrens are placed at their nests, if that cannot be done,

[72] Ducks and cranes are meant.

[73] Described as large and small clumps of adobe mud, formed by beating rains (Sandoval).

simply near the rocks, but a running ledge of rocks[74] should not be selected. The White Butterfly (prayersticks) are placed in level, open flats.

155. May he recover in good condition, may he go about without sickness of any kind, may he go about immune to sickness!
Let the path before him be pleasant! Let the path behind him be pleasant! Let the path below him be pleasant! Let the path above him be pleasant! Let all his surroundings be pleasant! Let every word of his mouth be pleasant!
Let him walk about as one who is Long-life Happiness One!
Pleasant it has become again! (four times).

156. This one should say when one has made all offerings, then one starts to return home. While carrying the prayerstick along, a person does not speak to those whom he meets; even though they address him, he should make no reply. Should the prayerstick be broken while it is being carried for an offering, it is not deposited (offered) in that condition, but is carried back to be repaired. Only then it may be deposited.

157. If a person has (much) regard for these prayersticks, he places something under each one of them to have them prepared on it. This will be something like a piece of calico or, instead, some money, from two bits up to a dollar.[75] You see, with us Navajos, if one should be dying for want of it[76] and should ask (a singer) for his songs, and (the latter) gives the information, he thereby wins from him (the pupil). Thus if a pupil starts out with his (singer's) songs he thereby acquires property, (and) he wins four times from him.[77] After that he (the pupil) himself may do with it as he pleases. Then, as time goes on, the instructor does not conceal points from him which may be lacking, but tells him from time to time. In this way we Navajo practice the singings which were laid down for us. Therefore we say that it is the Long-life Happiness One. Behind them[78] we go along, increasing. That is the way it really is, my Granduncle!

[74]A bluff or solid rock mass should not be selected, but a place where the rocks are broken and scattered.

[75]This passage refers to the patient, but the following part of the text seems to refer to the pupil.

[76]Anxious to learn, to become a singer.

[77]Reference is to the first four singings after apprenticeship. The earnings from these should be given to the instructor. Nowadays this custom is no longer observed (Sandoval).

[78]Chants in general, not only this particular one (Sandoval).

PART TWO: THE NAVAJO TEXT

1. Tooji hwiidzoh asdzą́ą́, asdzą́ą́ dishch'idí bił

1. Díí tóeeígíí tooji hwiidzoh hoolyéédóó sáanii naaki áádóó há'áazhii bits'ą́ą́dóó deezt'i'ii át'é. Ła' éí tooji hwiidzoh asdzą́ą́ wolyé; ła' asdzą́ą́ dishch'idí. Bee bił ééhózinii t'áá yit'įį́ lá, jiní. Nílch'i áłts'íísí wóne'é ndaajeehígíí éí bee bił ééhózin lá. Naaki, ła' biką'ii, ła' bi'áadiigo, éí yit'įį́ lá, jiní.

2. Nadahaaz'ái[1] hoolyéédóó hahóolįįdii, éí beiyiszįįd, jiní. Jó łahgo át'éego ntséskees, sitsóóké, ní jiní. Ákwe'é ła' diné yídéeshkił deidoołtséét shį́į́, ní jiní. Nílch'i áłts'íísí yę́ę biką' nilíinii yá'ąąshgóó dah bidiil'a', jiní. Éí ákódei íiyá. Áadi shį́į́ yá'ąąshdi níłtsą́ ashkii índa níłtsą́ at'ééd yaa níyá. Áadi yaa níyáago k'os diłhił yee bighan[2] lá, jiní. K'os dootł'izh yee bighan lá, jiní. K'os łitso yee bighan lá, jiní. K'os łigai yee bighan lá, jiní. Atsiniltł'ish yit'įį́ lá, jiní. Hatsoo' yilghał yit'įį́ lá, jiní. Shá bitł'óól yit'įį́ lá, jiní. Nááts'íilid yit'įį́ lá, jiní. T'áá náánà bee bił ééhózinii hólǫ́ǫ́ lá, dootso diłhił, dootso dootł'izh, dootso łitso, dootso[3] łigai bee hólǫ́ǫ́ lá jiní.

3. Díí kodóó shį́į́, Ha'át'éego baa ntsíníkees dooleeł, hojiní jiní. Níłtsą́ ashkii, níłtsą́ at'ééd binaalchí'í yę́ę yich'į' haadzíí', jiní. Ha'a'aahjígo dah diilyeed, yiłní jiní. Ii'ni' diłhił éí binífníí', ní jiní. Áadi yah yílwod, jiní. K'os diłhił yee náábighan lá, jiní. Atsiniltł'ish

[1] White Singer suggests *nooda haz'ái*, a kind of yucca *(nooda)* covering the side of this mountain in the Apache country. I am rendering Yucca Mountain.

[2] *Bighan*, his hogan made of cloud, not: *bee kin*, house of cloud. *Bighan* can be rendered "his home," although one could expect *bee kin*, his house of, if this were a story of Pueblo origin.

[3] *Dootso*, a white-faced fly, larger than the house fly. This informant does not nasalize *dǫǫtso*.

bidáádińláá lá, jiní. Tó bits'áneeltiingo sitįį lá, jiní. T'óó ninishníi'go ásht'į. Níłtsą ashkii, hágo, niłní, bijiní jiní. T'ąą' dah ńdiilwod, jiní. Nálwod, jiní. Áádęę' dah deesdee', ní jiní. Nááná shádi'ááhjí ii'ni' dootł'izh, k'os dootł'izh yee bighan lá. Hatsoo yilghał bidáádińláá lá. Tó bits'áneeltiingo sitįį lá, jiní. Dah ńdiilwod, ninááńálwod. Aadęę' dah deesdee', ní jiní.

4. E'e'aahjí dah náádiilwod. Ii'ni' łitso k'os łitso yee bighango shá bitł'óól bidáádińláá lá. Tó bits'áneeltiingo sitįį lá, jiní. Aadóó dah nínáádiilwodii nálwod. Aadęę' k'ad dah deesdee', ní jiní. Náhookǫsjí dah náádiilwod. Éí ááji ii'ni' łigai k'os łigai yee bighan lá. Náátsʼíílid bidáádinílá́á lá. Tó bits'áneeltiingo sitįį lá, jiní. Dah nínáádiilwodii nínáánálwod. Aadęę' k'ad dah deesdee', ní jiní.

5. Ii'ni' diłhiłígíí éí bigáál hólǫǫ lá, jiní, níłch'i diłhił bigáál lá, jiní. Ii'ni' dootł'izh níłch'i dootł'izh bigáál lá, jiní. Ii'ni' łitso níłch'i łitso bigáál lá, jiní. Ii'ni' łigai níłch'i łigai bigáál lá, jiní. Ahaneheeskai, jiní. Háí lá dooleeł lá, tooji hwiidzohjį' dah náhodidooleeł lá, ní jiní. Díí ii'ni' dįį'goígíí yaa yádaałti'.[4] Háí lá dooleeł lá, ní jiní. Níłtsą ashkii kwe'é ałghazdeest'ą, jiní. Ákohgo shá bitł'áh jiłchíí', ashkii nilįįgo. Éí bee há'oodzíí', jiní. Ni lá k'ad ákóyah dah hodidííleeł. Ni tooji hwiidzoh asdzą́ą́ baa hodííleeł, hojiní jiní. Lą'ąą, jiní jiní.

6. Kodóó dah náhodiileehdóó náátsʼíílid beehétł'ááh ałnániildéelii ákóyah dahodiileeh, jiní. Tooji hwiidzoh asdzą́ą́ baa hozhnílįįd, jiní. Yoołgaii bee bighan lá, jiní. Yoołgaii bá hásteel lá, jiní. Índa dootł'izh yee bighan lá, jiní. Dootł'izhii bá hásteel lá, jiní. Diichiłí yee bighan lá, jiní. Diichiłí bá hásteel lá, jiní. Bááshzhinii yee bighan lá jiní. Bááshzhinii bá hásteel lá, jiní. Díí ntł'iz yee bighango dziiłtsánęę éí t'óó hoł ádzaa lá, jiní. Hazhó'ó jinééł'įį', ńt'éé' hojooba' náhoot'a', jiní. T'áá áłtsééd ąą' át'éhęęgi anádzá, jiní.

7. Ákohgo shįį t'óó t'įįhígo nahjį' náhizhdeezhtłizhígi dootsoh hastiin haa náánálwod, jiní. T'áá ákǫǫ honílǫ k'ad. T'áá nee' yit'ée doo. Shí díí t'óó ásht'į; t'óó nijeeh hash'aah, hojiní jiní. Dįį' yiskąągo át'éé lá, jiní, Díí baa hwiińt'įįgo. Daa léit'éé lá, ní jiní tooji hwiidzoh asdzánęę. Tó názbąs hoolyé jiilaa. Shíni' ájiilaa ndi ka nisin, ní jiní, tooji hwiidzoh asdzą́ą́. Be'ek'id hóteelí hoolyé: díí t'áá ahąąh áhoolyé. Áaji la' ntséskees, ní jiní.

[4] *Baa yádaałti'*, you discuss it, would be clearer (Sandoval).

2. Nanise' bee bighan

8. Bini'ant'ą́ą́'tsózí bini'ant'ą́ą́'tsoh bił ałch'į' heezláagi yaa ńdaat'į́, jiní, nanise' ałtso hadidzaagi. Náátsʼíílid yit'įį́ lá jiní. Éí yideezdéelgo bikáá' adeesdee', jiní, áajį'. Łahjí tó názbąs hoolyéego, łahjí be'ek'id hóteel hoolyéego bita'gi nizhńdéél, jiní. Ákwe'é nizhńdéelgo t'áá áko, Wehee, ńléí tó názbąs hoolyéejį' dah diináah, sitsóí, hojiní jiní. Ha'át'íí biniiyé, shichó, bijiní jiní. Díí k'ai dootł'izh naakigo ńdííjih índa k'aiłchíí' ałdó' naakigo ńdííjih, hałní jiní. Éí aazhníyáago ájiilaa, jiní. K'ai dootł'izhí naaki índa k'aiłchíí' naaki náázhńjaa' jiní.

9. Be'ek'id hóteeljį' náádíídááł, sitsóí, hałní jiní. Ha'át'íí biniiyé, shichó, bijiní jiní. Díí teeł náhást'éigo ńdííjih, hałní jiní. Ákohgo shįį́ éí nínáázhníjaa'. Áko nahgóó t'óó sinil, jiní. Níłch'i hwee ééhózinęęę áhojiní jiní, Ńlááhdęę́' diné bida'íłnii', ha'át'éego nihá yaa nínáá-dóot'įįł, hojiní jiní. Biką'ii nilínęęę ha'a'aahjigo dah diilwod jiní. Dólii dine'é yaa yílwod, hane' yeiní'ą́, jiní. Bi'áadii nilínęęę e'e'aahjį' dah diilwod, jiní. Níłtsą́dlǫ́ǫ́' dine'é yaa yílwod, jiní. Hane' yeiní'ą́, jiní. Dólii dine'é yęęę dinégo neheeskai, jiní. Índa níłtsą́dlǫ́ǫ́' dine'é yęęę dinégo neheeskai, jiní.

10. Díí yee' bee shighan doogo, éí biniiyé ádishní, sitsóóké, ní jiní, tooji hwiidzoh asdzą́ą́ asdzą́ą́ dishch'idí yiłgo ání jiní. Lą́'ąą, daaní jiní. Dólii dine'é yęęę ha'a'aahdęę́'go niikai, jiní. K'ai dootł'izhii yęęę ńdeidiitą́, jiní. Níłtsą́dlǫ́ǫ́' dine'é yęęę shádi'ááhdęę́' k'aiłchíí' dine'é ńdeidiitą́, jiní. E'e'aahdęę́' dólii dine'é yęęę k'ai dootł'izhí ła' nínáá-deidiitą́, jiní. Náhookǫsdęę́' níłtsą́dlǫ́ǫ́' dine'é k'aiłchíí'ęę ła' nínáá-deidiitą́, jiní. Ałch'į' deestsih, jiní, bee hooghan ályaa. Ha'a'aahdęę́' dólii dine'é teełdęę́' ńdeidiilá, jiní. Shádi'ááhdęę́' níłtsą́dlǫ́ǫ́' dine'é teeł ńdeidiilá; e'e'aahdęę́' índa náhookǫsdęę́' t'áá ákódzaa. T'áá łahjį' teełęęę

hooghan yee deíshjéé', jiní. Ákone' shįį́ índa t'áá dį́į́'dę́ę́' ch'ilátah hózhǫ́ǫ́ niilchį́, jiní. Éí shįį́ teełę́ę bikáa'gi ts'ídá ałtso yaago bilátahgo hooghan béhééshjéé', bik'ehgo níłtsą́ą́jí naagháa doo biniiyé, jiní. Hooghan niilts'id ha'a'aahjį' ch'íhoodzą́ągo. Ahéhee' lą́, sitsóóké, hooghan shá ńdasoo'ą́, jiní jiní.

11. Kwe'é lá ntł'iz hataas'nii'. Dólii biką'ii dootł'izhii biyeel ályaa, jiní. Índa dólii bi'áadii yoołgaii biyeel ályaa, jiní. Índa níłtsą́dlǫ́ǫ́' biką'ii diichiłí biyeel ályaa, jiní. Índa bi'áadii nilíinii bááshzhinii biyeel ályaa, jiní jiní.

3. Dich'ízhí nahodidáhí

12. Ákohgo shį́į́, Díí tó názbąs t'áá bíighahjígo ha'a'aah bich'ijį' ahozhniitáál, ńlóee, ho'doo'niid jiní. K'adshą'[5] ii'ni' dilhil hastiin ahoniitáál lá, jiní. Ákohgo ńlááhjí k'ad hastói yah íiyáago kojí ałdó' hó ndzíiztą́, jiní. Hachóhę́ę dííí hooghanii shádi'ááhjígo siké, jiní. Hó éí náhookǫsjí jishjool, t'óó yę́ę jichǫ́ǫgo. Ákohgo shį́į́ ńlááhdę́ę́' háajį' há ádayiilaa; ayáásh dine'é hooghan ádayiilaaą́ą t'áá ałtso dich'ízhí, dahałní jiní. Índa nahodidáhí, dahałní jiní. Ákohgo shį́į́ kojí jishjoolgo hanaashjí tł'oh ts'ózí yiistł'ǫ́ǫ'go yee niljoł. Ákohgo shį́į́ tł'ée'go haa saad bíghą́ą' lá, jiní, ájít'ée dooleełgi yeińt'į́įgo. Áko hó éí ch'ééh bik'izhdiitįįh, jiní, t'áá biyi'ídi ałch'į' yáłti'go.

13. Hayíílką́, jiní. Hashkézhniidzį́į', jiní. Yáadi lá doo haa hasht'eenééh shį́į beinóot'į, ndiiyołhosh ni', bijiní jiní. Yoó, sitsói, t'áadoo ádíníní. Áńt'ée dooleełgi beiníit'į, hałní jiní. Ałtso hoos'įįd jiní. T'áá áko ndi t'áá łahgóó chahałheeł naaz'ą́, jiní. Bee nihaa nánt'įį ndi, sitsói, ńléí ndidlídii binaa ńdiilyeed, hałní jiní. Dooda yéé', shił hóyéé'. T'áásh doo biniiyéhígóó náázhdiilwod doo, jiní jiní. T'áadoo ádíníní, sitsói, shi'awéé', binaa ńdidíílwołígíí. Éí łį́į́' át'éego, hałní jiní.

[5] *K'adshą'.... lá*, that, it happened, was....

4. Dishch'id yee hahodiila

14. Binaa nízhdiilwod, jiní. Ńjílwod, jiní. T'áá shį́į́ áko asdzą́ą́ dishch'idí yę́ę haadzíí', jiní. Kwe'é yiizį', sitsóí, hałní jiní. T'áá shį́į́ áko dishch'id hoolyéii yee hahodiila, jiní. Yił hakáá' ndeesnii', jiní.

15. Áko ńlááhjí ach'į' didooljéé', jiní. Hakáá' niníkę́ę́z, hadááh ńdeizǫ́ǫ́z, hanaa da. K'ad ńlááh hatáálgóó dínááh, sitsóí. Deit'áo nadló doogą́ą́ł, hałní jiní. Aadóó shį́į́ t'áá áko dashdiiyá ákóó. Hatááldóó kojígo ha'a'aah bich'ijígo nda'azhǫǫsh lá, jiní. Yé'ii dine'é nda'azhǫǫsh lá, jiní. Ayaash dine'é nda'azhǫǫsh lá, jiní. Hashch'éé̱łti'í yoołgaii binaa azhǫǫsh lá, jiní. Hashch'éoghan dootł'izhii binaa azhǫǫsh lá, jiní. Nináda'a zhǫǫshgi jineezdá, jiní, t'óó ahayóigi ájít'éego. Hádą́ą́' lá ákójít'éego nda'azhǫǫshgi dzizdá. Ńláahdi nínááh áko t'óó naa'iih, dahałní jiní. T'óó bik'ee yaa ádzaa, doo hadzoodzíí' da, jiní. Aadóó dah náázdiidzá, jiní. E'e'aah bich'ijigo ch'iyáán ál'íńę́ędi nádzídzá, jiní. Dólii ch'ikéí, tsídiiłtsoi ch'ikéí, tashchizh dootł'izh ch'ikéí, chozhghálii ch'ikéí, nahoodlǫ́ǫ́'[6] ch'ikéí, níłtsą́dlǫ́ǫ́' ch'ikéí, hasbídí ch'ikéí, ákohgo ch'iyáán yaa naakai.

16. T'áá éí diné łahjí nda'azhǫǫsh, jiní. Haniinaa doo áajį' dadikáah da, jiní, daha'į́įgo. Ha'át'éego lá hatáaljį' náádeeshdááł lá. Diné la' dashi'į, dziniizį́į́'. Shichó bee bił hodeeshnih, shá iidoonih, jiniizį́į́', jiní. T'áá shį́į́ áko haghangóó dah nízdiidzá, jiní. Híiłch'į'go ńdzídzá, jiní. Ya'ałníi'gi néidzįįh, sitsóí, jiní asdzą́ą́ dishch'idí. Ha'a'aahdę́ę́'go ch'il niiníłchį́į́ lá, jiní. Ts'ídá ałtso yilátahí áyiilaa lá jiní. Éí yił hodeesnii'. Łóódę́ę ałtso hą̨ąh náálʼdááz, jiní.

[6] Also *nahadlǫ́ǫ́'*, but this is described by one informant as a lizard, fleet and crystal colored, the size of an index finger (listed as small lizard in *Navajo English Vocabulary* on page 122).

17. Tooji hwiidzohgi tooji hwiidzoh asdzą́ą́ dishch'id[7] *niyeel áshłaa,*
Yoołgaii nizhóní niyeel áshłaa, t'eeshchii nizhónii niyeel áshłaa, tádídíín dootł'izh nizhónii niyeel áshłaa, tádídíín nizhónii niyeel áshłaa.
Ni'álíil shá háádíílééł, ni'álíil shá háánéínílá,
Sits'ą́ąjį' dah ńdidíílééł, nízaagóó sits'ą́ néínílá.
Hózhǫ́ǫgo náázhdidoodááł,[8] *hózhǫ́ǫgo ch'ízhdoogááł, hózhǫ́ǫgo njigháa doo, doo hąąh tééhgóó*[9] *njigháa doo, doo hohodééł-níígóó njigháa doo,*[10]
Hatsiįį' hózhǫ́ǫgo njigháa doo, hakéédę́ę́' hózhǫ́ǫgo njigháa doo.
Są'ah naagháí bik'eh hózhóón jílįįgo njigháa doo,
Hózhǫ́ laaká,[11] *hózhǫ́ laaká, hózhǫ́ náhásdlįį́', hózhǫ́ náhásdlįį́'.*

18. Aajį' shįį ákódzaa. Naaki tł'éé' nahodoogaałgo t'áá ákǫ́ǫ́ náájíshjool índa hachó hanaashiijí haa saad náábíígháą́' ndi doo bik'izhdiitįįh da. Ńlááhdę́ę́' hayííłkááago aajį' bee baa nínáádzíst'įįd. Ha'át'íí lá baa saad nihighą́, ni'iiyoołhoshee, bijiní jiní. Adą́ądą́ą́' lá diné shaa tsi' dahodeest'i' ni'. Ha'át'íí shįį bee hashidoołaago diné shaa tsí dadeesdloh, bijiní jiní. Jó t'áadoo ádíníní, sitsóí, áńt'ée dooleełgi ná baa yéiilti', hałní jiní. Ńléí díwózhiiłbáí binaa ńdidíílwoł, hałní jiní. Áko lá bił nsininii', shił hóyéé', bijiní jiní. Áko lá binaa ńdinilwodgo, éí dibé át'ée ni, sitsóí, hałní jiní.

[7]Instead of *dishch'id* substitute in the three other prayers the following words: *Nákid*, Spanish pock, syphilis, *azee', nchįhii*, poisonous. *(Nchį'ii)*, dragon's head sage. *K'ishishjíízh* (nettle) and alternate *shikéédę́ę́' sitsiįį'* for second and fourth prayer.

[8]The forms here rendered should properly be in the first singular as patient is supposed to repeat the words: *náádideeshdááł*, I will recover, let me recover. *Ch'ídeeshááł*, I will walk out, *doo shąąh tééhgóó naasháa doo* nothing preventive on me let me go about. *Doo shihodééłníígóó* insensitive to disease let me go about. *Sitsiįį', shikéédę́ę́' są'ah naagháí nishłį́įgo naasháa doo.*

[9]*Doo hąąh tééhgóó*, let him go about in perfect health.

[10]*Ho* (*hodééłní*, it affects him) everything, he is sensitive to it, reduplicated *ho* gives the word a sort of passive sense: immune, insensitive to all sickness.

[11]One informant explains that this is the original form for *hózhǫ́ náhásdlįį́'* used by Talking-god in the *hózhǫ́ǫ́jí* rite. But here both forms are used.

5. Nákid yee hanááhodiidla

19. Éí binaa nízhdiilwod, jiní, aadę́ę́' hayíílkáągo ńjílwod, jiní. Ya'ałníi'gi náánéidzį́įh, hałní jiní. Éí áajį' náádziidzį́įhgo ákwe'é nákid yee hanááhodiidla. K'ad ákǫ́ǫ́ náádíídááh, sitsóí. Hán ninááadajoodloh, sitsóí, hałní jiní. Éí áadi ńléí nda'azhǫǫshę́ędi nádzídzá, jiní. Niná-da'azhǫǫshdóó náázneezdá. Áko díí t'óó ahayóigi ájít'éego t'óó yaa ájít'éego dzizdá, jiní. Ákóyaii yówehdi ninaá dich'ízhí nahodidáhí dandooshǫsh da, hałní jiní. Aadóó dah náázdiidzá, jiní. Éí ńléí ch'iyáán ál'íńę́ędi nádzídzá, jiní. Yáadi lá, bee ádoolníił nihich'į' dah yigháah t'óó baa'iihgo yówehdi nínááh, t'áadoo nihich'į' dah nínáhí, ho'doo'niid jiní.

20. Ha'át'íishą', ha'át'éego lá diné ayóigo shá dadoolni, jiniizį́'ii hatáaljį' dashdiiyá, jiní. Ch'é'etiindę́ę́' nizhníyá, jiní. Ha'át'íí shį́į óolyé naaskáą́'. Éí dáádiníbaal lá, jiní. Ąą ájiilaa, jiní, shádi'ááh bich'ijigo. Ńt'éé' wóniidi sitį, jiní, hataałii. Aadóó kojí ła' naháaztą́, jiní. Yáadi lá bee ádoołníił. Éí ga' léi' baa náháne' yówehjį' dabidoo'nínę́ęni, jiní jiní, hataałii jílíinii. Ha'át'éego lá áníí lá, jiniizį́', jiní. K'ad bee hazdoodzihgo łahjígo ąą anáájiidlaa, jiní. Ńt'éé'[12] naakits'áadah baa ákéé' lá jiní. Hak'éé yaa ádaadzaa, jiní.

21. T'áá shį́į áko dah nízdiidzá. Éí ńléidi ńjídzá híiłch'į'ígo hachó sikéhę́ędi. Shádi'ááhdę́ę'go ch'ilátah hózhóón bilátahí ninéeníłchį́į lá, jiní. Éí yił hakáá' ninááadeesnii', łóódę́ę ałtso hąąh ninááńááłdááz, jiní.

[12]The sentence seems incomplete "when he was about to speak he raised the curtain of the hogan on the other side (north)." *Nt'éé'* may mean "when," or "but he didn't," because he noticed the twelve wives of the singer who bowed their heads being ashamed of him.

Áajį' hąąh ásdįįdgo hach'į' haadzíí', jiní. Ha'át'íí ni'doo'niid, sitsóí, ní jiní. Ha'át'íí lá shi'didoo'niił. K'ad t'óó lá diné shá ńdahast'i' ni'; diné shaa daadloh, deidoolzhǫǫd ni', bijiní jiní. Lą́'ąą, sitsóí, daa niit'ée dooleeł, ńlááh, jiní.[13] Íłhosh, hałní jiní. T'áá áko aajį' dah nízdiidzáayii náázhneeshjool, jiní.

22. Aadóó ńlááhjí haa yájiłti'go néidiiską́, jiní. Doo bik'izh'diitįįh da jiní. Ńlááhdę́ę́' hayííłką́ągo bee baa nínáádzíst'įįd, jiní. Yáadi lá bee ádoolnííł, yáadi lá baa saad nihighą́. Ni'iiyołhóósh nihiniinaa yee' shibił hishníísh, doo ashhosh da, bijiní jiní. Yoó, sitsóí, t'áadoo ádíníní, áńt'ée dooleełgi beiniit'į, hałní jiní. Áko lá t'óó diné shaa daadloh ni'. Shaa dloh dadilzhǫ́ǫ ni', bijiní jiní. T'áadoo ádíníní, sitsóí, ńléí chá'oł binaa nínáádiilyeed, náhodi'ní jiní. Éí binaa ńdiishwodgosh, ha'át'íí shaa doodił, bijiní jiní. Jó yódí át'éii, sitsóí, hałní jiní. Binaa nízhdiilwod ńjílwod, jiní. Kwe'e k'ad ya'ałnii'gi ninááníilyeed, sitsóí, hałní jiní. K'ad háni' ni naa dajoodloh. Daa ná yit'ée doo, sitsóí, hałní jiní.

[13]*Ńláăh háni'*, go on now and don't let it worry you, would be better here than *ńlááji ni*.

6. Azee nichį'ii yee hanááhodiidla

23. Azee nichį'ii yee hanááhodiidla, jiní. Haa'íshą' ákǫ́ǫ́ náádídááh ńlááh, sitsóí, hałní jiní. Hakáá' ninááníkę́ęzgo aadóó ákǫ́ǫ́ náádzídzáhígíí ninááda'ashzhǫǫshę́ęgi náázneezdá, jiní. Yáadi lá bee ádoolníił nihaa náánádzá, t'óó baa'ihgo. Yówehdi naniná héí dich'íjí nahodidáhí. T'áadoo nihich'į' dah nínáhí, náho'doo'niid jiní. Dandooshǫǫsh da. T'óó yá'ájít'éego dzizdá, jiní. Aadóó shįį́ t'áá áko dah náázdiidzáhí ch'iyáán ál'įįdi náádzídzá. Yáadi lá bee ádoolníił, t'óó baa'ihę́ę nihaa náánádzá náádaho'doo'niid aadóó t'óó dah nínáázdiidzá. Hatálę́ę t'óó bich'éédą́ą́'góó ts'éédzídzá. Hachó sikéhę́ędi nínáádzídzá, jiní.

24. Ya'ałnii'gi náánéidzįįh, sitsóí, hałní jiní. E'e'aahdę́ę́' ch'ilátah hózhóón bilátahí nínáánéiniłchįį́' lá. Hąąh ánááyiidlaa, hąąh nináánáłdááz, jiní. Sitsóí, ha'át'íí nááńdoo'niid ha'át'éego naa náhwiinínst'įįd, hałní jiní. Diné lá t'óó shaa daaldloh ni'. Diné lá t'óó shá ndahałt'i' ni'. Shaa dloh deidoolzhǫǫd, náábizhdoo'niid jiní. Lą́'ąą, sitsóí, daa neít'ée doo ńlááhjí náá'íłhosh, hałní jiní.

25. Náázneeztį, jiní. Nahjí hanaashiijí hachóhę́ę ałch'į' nááneeshjool, jiní. Aadóó shįį́ áajį' saad yaa náádiit'áázh. Haa saad náábíígháą́'go yoołkááł. Hayíiłką́ baa nínáádzíst'įįd. Ha'át'íí yówéh át'éego bił ndi doo nohsin da lá, ni'iiyoołhóóshee'. Nihiniinaa doo hazhǫ́'ó ashhosh da, bijiní jiní. Yoó, sitsóí, shą́ą́' t'áadoo ádíníní, ndishní, daa nee át'éego, sitsóí, hałní jiní. Áko lá ńléí gad binaa nínáádiilyeed, hałní jiní. Áko lá bił łikanii shił hóyéé', bijiní jiní. Áko lá ni nínáádiilyeed ni', sitsóí, shi'awéé', hałní jiní. Ákosh éí binaa ńdiishwodgosh ha'át'íí át'é, bijiní jiní. T'áadoo ádíníní, sitsóí, ntł'iz át'é, hałní jiní. Éí binaa nínáázhdiilwod gadę́ę, nínáájilwod, jiní. T'áá áko, kwe'é ya'ałnii'gi ninááńilyeed, sitsóí, hałní jiní.

7. K'íshíshjįįzh yee hanááhodidla

26. K'íshíshjįįzh hakáá' yił nináádeesnii'go t'óó ahayóigo hakáá' ninááníkę́ę́z jiní. Haa shįį lá hą́ą ákóó náádídááh, nda'azhǫǫshgóó hatáálgóó, náho'doo'niid jiní. Índa díí na'azhǫǫshgi doo díníidaał da. T'áá át'é hatah tádidíinaał índa ch'iyáán ál'į́įgi t'áá át'é hatah tádidíinaał índa hatáál góne' yah adíínááł, hodííniid jiní. Aadóó áá náádzídzá, jiní. Haa nínáádaniidloh índa há nináádahałt'i', jiní T'áá áko ndi diné bitaajighááh, jiní hak'ee nahondzood, jiní. Hatáál góne' yah ajííyá, jiní. T'óó k'asídą́ą́' dzineezdá, hojishchį, jiní, asdzání yę́ę. Ałtso hats'ą́ąjį'[14] dineezbin, jiní. T'áá shįį áko áádóó nikéédzídzá, hííłch'į'go ńdzídzá, jiní. Ya'ałnii'gi nínínááh, sitsóí, hałní jiní.

27. Náhookǫsdę́ę́'go ch'ilátah hózhóón bilátahí nínááneiníłchįį' lá, jiní. Éí yił hakáá' nináádeesnii'. Ałtso hakáá' ninááďiiłdááz, jiní. Ą́ą', sitsóí, ha'át'íí náándoo'niid, hałní jiní. K'ad diné lá t'óó shá ndahast'i' ni'. Diné shaa dloh deidoozhǫ́ǫ́', bijiní jiní. Lą́'ąą, sitsóí, jó ákót'éé lá. Azhą́ lá ákót'ee ndi bee hoł ééhózinii hólǫ́ǫ ndi doo azhdoonih da dootsoh diłhił.

28. T'įįhdígo yaa adeez'ą́ągo níłch'i áłts'íísí yę́ę ha'a'aahjigo dah diil'a'. Níłch'i diłhił bi'ílnii'. Azhą́ lá shí ts'aa' yisht'įį ndi, shí dooda, t'áá hó ájít'į tooji hwiidzoh asdzą́ą́ jílíinii. Kót'éego níłch'i biyázhí hane' néiní'ą́, jiní. Yisht'įį lá, ní jiní. Ha'a'aahjį' dah diiyá, jiní. T'áá bí asdzánę́ę táláwosh dįį' bik'eh áníłtsogo hayíítą́ą́ lá, jiní. Ákwe'é naską́ą́' niilkaad jiní. Táláwoshę́ę bikáa'gi taosnii', jiní. Bee tá'ázdeesgiz, jiní, ts'ídá t'áá át'é. Yoołgaii bee náhodooltsai, jiní.

[14] *Hats'ą́ąjį' dineezbin*, turned their backs on him (sitting), because they were probably seated when he entered.

8. Hataałii baazhdíílá silį́į́'

29. Ákwe'é hachó akéédę́ę́' nilínęę kǫ́ǫ́ naskáá' ninááda'iiskaad, bikáá'góó yoołgaii nii'nil, jiní. K'ad naskáá'ąą bikáá'góó tsé'yaa nteeh, hałní jiní. Hatah dahodeests'ǫǫd, jiní, hadoh da dah naaznilgo áyiilaa, jiní. Hatsii' ńléí hatah hazhooshjį' yił ndeelnii', jiní. Yoołgaii yee hahodiila, jiní. Yoołgaii haadaat'é, hatáá' niiní'ą́, jiní. Yoołgaii hatsii' bee jishtłish[15] nahalingo áyiilaa, jiní. Tsíłkę́ęhgo nízhdii'na', jiní. Hats'á hodidichiłgo nízhdii'na', jiní. Díí éí k'ad bik'ehgo naninúa doo, sitsóí, shi'awéé', ho'doo'niid. Níłch'i biyázhí yę́ę ałch'ijí hajaat'ah dah hiszid. Shí la' ałdó' ákónísht'é ni, sitsóí. T'áá shį́į́ ákóhodíílíiłgo át'é, hałní jiní.

30. Áko ńlááhjí ła'atł'éé' hojitaał, jiní. Ńlááh, sitsóí, ákǫ́ǫ́ dínááh, nik'ee daats'í yaa ninááádazhnt'aah doo. Nik'ee daats'í ninááhondzood doo, hałní jiní. Aadóó dashdiiyá, jiní, akǫ́ǫ́. Diyin dine'é índa ayáásh dine'é, asdzání da t'óó ahayóigo ałah silį́į́' lá, jiní. Áadizhníyá, jiní. Tł'óógóó tázhdígháah, jiní. Ałjeeh ńdanilnii', jiní. Ha'át'íí lá diné shį́į́ níyáá lá, t'óó la' baa yáhásin, daaní jiní. Aadę́ę́' yah ajííyá jiní. Há ąą ályaayii hataałii sidáí bikéé'dóó há hoo'a', jiní. Doo hak'i daaghaał da, hak'ee yaa ndaat'aah, jiní. Haa yá daninízin, jiní. Baa akéé ayóí adanoolni lá, jiní. Yah ííjéé' ńláahjį', hak'éé daaghałgo ch'éédadildloh, jiní. T'áá áko ts'aa' yaa aniitą́, jiní. Ła'atł'éé'[16] hojíítáál, jiní. Ts'aa'

[15]*Bee jishtłish*, rammed down, that is, completely covered with beads, perhaps "pressed into the hair with the hands."

[16]*Ła'atł'éé' hojíítáál*, the first night of tapping the basket-drum, which is the fifth night of a nine-night ceremony (or first of a five-night ceremony).

deniilt'e', jiní, aadóó tł'óógóó dah nízdiidzáago bi'ąą[17] nandeehęę hakéé' dah ahidíníilchąą' lá jiní. Bił hwiiską, jiní. Ałk'ééjii'nil, jiní. Áko shįį hataałii yęę baazhdíílá silįį'.

31. Ńdzídzá hachó sikéedi. Daa hoot'é, sitsóí, ní jiní. Hataałii baa díílá, jiní jiní. Áko lá át'é dishní ni, sitsóí, hałní jiní. Índa naskąą'ąą há niilkaad bikáá'góó jineeztį jiní. Ła' hak'iilkaad, jiní, ádąąh ńjíbįį'go. Éí shįį[18] t'óó da'jiłhoshgo yiską. Ńlááhdęę' hayííłkąągo, Nínáádiilyeed, sitsóí, hałní jiní. T'áá éí binaa nínáázhdiilwod, jiní, ńdílídii. Nínáájílwodgo dootł'izhiits'aa' biyi' tánáhodisgiz, tsá'ászi' ntsaaígíí bee. Dootł'izhii bee nínáhodooltsai.

32. Éí ákohgo doolyaago t'áá áko t'óó ádá hozhdilyingo njigháago t'áá íiyisí hidideeshch'į', jiní. Dootł'izhii yęę bee hanááhodilyaa, jiní. K'ad ákǫǫ náádíídááh, sitsóí, hałní jiní. Áá náádzídzá, jiní. T'óó nahgóó tł'óógóó ninráádzízį', jiní. T'áá ákót'éego ałjeeh nínáádanilnii', jiní. Há'ąą ánáánályaayii yah anáádzoodzá, hataałii bikee' góne' há náához'a'. Áádóó nááznee zdá. Baa akéé yęę hanaashiijí náánál'ááh. T'áá áko ts'aa' yaa nináánátą, naaki tł'éé' hojíítáál. Dah náázdiidzá, ts'aa' deniilt'e'go. Táá' hakéé' dah diijéé'. T'áá bíighah bił náhwiiską, jiní. Naaki tł'éé' azlįį'go ashdla' ajíínil.

33. T'áá shįį áko aadóó dah nínáázdiidzá, ńléidi hachóhęę baa nínáádzídzá. Daa ánít'įįd, sitsóí, náho'doo'niid jiní, áadi. Hataałii lá baa díínílaa ni. Táá' lá bił náásiiskąą ni, jiní jiní. Yá'át'ééh lá, áko lá ádííníił biniiyé naninishtin ni', sitsóí, hałní jiní. T'áá shįį áko ha'át'íí shįį óolyé bik'i ndzisgai, há nináánálkaad, háazhdiijaa'. T'óó bikáá'góó nááhwiiską; ńlááhjí ałdó' hachó náábiiską, jiní.

34. Hayííłkąągo, K'ad nahdęę' nínáádiilyeed, sitsóí, hałní jiní. T'áá áłtséédąą' binaa nízhdiilwodęę díwózhiiłbáí binaa nínáázhdiilwod, nínáájílwod jiní. T'áá áłtséédąą' yęęgi anáánádzá. Diichiłíts'aa' biyi' tsá'ázits'óóz bee tánáhodisgiz, jiní. Diichiłí bee nínááhodooltsai, jiní. T'áá ákǫǫ t'óó ninráájídáahgo t'áá hazhó'ó híiłch'į'go diichiłí bee hanáhodilyaa, jiní. T'áá áko tágí tł'éé' hojitaałgo dah náázdiidzá. Áá náádzídzá t'óó nahgóó diné bitaa náájídááh. Aadęę' yah anáádzoodzá, hataałii yęę bikéédóó há náhool'a'. Áko doo hahodeel'įįh da, jiní. Baa akéé yęę t'áá ałtso yah anáánájéé'. Ts'aa'ąą

[17] *Bi'ąą nandeehęę*, those that fell above that, here the two wives above ten, (of the singer's twelve wives).

[18] *Éí shįį*, that referring to what happens next morning, or "that done."

yah nínáánátą. Áko ńlááhdęę' hach'į' daadloh jiní. Ts'aa' de ninäánált'e'. Dah náádiijée'go bikéé'dóó dah náádiidzá. Táá' hakéé' dah náádiijéé' lá jiní. T'áá ałtso bił nááhwiiską.

35. Aadóó ńléidi hachóhęę baa nínáádzídzá. Ąą', sitsói, daa neinít'įįd, nááhodoo'niid jiní. Hataałii lá baa náádiishdlá ni, náázhdoo'niid. Áko lá ádíínííł biniiyé ni, sitsói, shi'awéé', ní jiní sáanii yęę. T'áá shįį áko ákwii diłhił naskąą' há ninäánálkaad bikáá' háázhdiijaa'. T'áá éí bikáá' nááhwiiską, jiní. Hachóhęę dó' t'áá ááji náábiiską. Doo kót'é da'ahizhdiinii da, jiní.

36. Hayíílkąągo, weehee', k'ad sitsói, nínáádiilyeed, ho'doo'niid. T'áá ałtséédąą' yęę binaa nínáázhdiilwod chá'oł. Éí aadęę' nínáájílwodgo bááshzhiniits'aa' há nináánátą. Táláwosh nináánályaa bee tánáhodisgiz; bááshzhinii bee nínááhodooltsai. T'áá áko ts'id łigaii há ninäánálkaad bikáádóó bááshzhinii bee hanááhodiilyaa. Ákohgo ńlááhjí dįį' tł'éé' hojitaał jiní. Ákǫǫ dah náázdiidzá. Áadi náádzídzá; t'óó ńlááhgóó ch'é'etiingóó ndzizį'. T'áá shįį áko yah anáádzoodzá, ńléí hataałii bíighahdi há náhoo'a'. Ńlááhjí asdzání yah anáánájéé', ts'aa' denáánált'e'. Ayáásh dine'é yęę diné danilíinii ałtso ch'ínááná-jée'go bikéé' asdzání ch'ínáánájéé'. Bikéé'dóó dah náázdiidzá. Naaki hakéé' dah nááhidíniilchąą' bił nááhwiiską.

37. Aadóó shįį hachóhęę baa nínáádzídzá. Daa yínít'įįd, sitsói, hałní jiní. Hataałii baa díílá, jiní jiní. T'áá ádzaagi danjózhíhęę dich'íjí danijinínęę nahodidáhí danijinínęę doo nizaa achaaní íínínil, hałní jiní hachó. T'ááłáhídi haadzíí', sitsói, shi'awéé'. K'ad ákǫǫ náá'íłhosh, hałní jiní. Ákohgo shįį t'óó nááhwiiską.

38. Hayíílkąągo, Ńlááh nínáádiilyeed, sitsói. T'ááłáhídi haadzíí', hałní jiní. Éí binaa nínáázhdiilwod gad, ńjílwodgo doo táninnear-hodisgiz da, jiní. Shá bihádídíín wolyéii t'éí hąąh ályaa. K'ad bíighah asíníłįį', hałní jiní. Díí nináájílwo'ęęjí bíighah azlįį'. Ákohgo shįį ńlááhjí bijį. Ákwii shįį shá bihádídíín t'éí hąąh ályaago, t'áá ákót'éego njigháago hííłch'į'go índa ntł'izęę ts'ídá t'áá át'é bee hahodiilyaa.

39. T'áá áko aajį' dashdiiyá, jiní, t'áá jįįgo. Áko ńléí diyin dine'é t'óó ahayóigo áłah silįį' lá, jiní. Áko ńléí diyin dine'é t'óó ahayóigo áłah silįį' lá, jiní. Áko ńléí bitaajigháahgo ąą kwáaniiłgo bitaajighá, jiní. Haa yá danízin diné. I'íí'ą, jiní. Áko t'áá ákǫǫ njighá, jiní. Yah anáájídááh, ch'ínáájídááh. Ákohgo shįį doo hah adidit'aahgóó[19] wónáásdóó ts'aa' yaa náánát'ą, jiní. Éí índa tł'éé' bíighah adoot'ááł. T'óó adoot'ááłjį' náázhnídah, jiní, t'áá kónízahíjį'. Éí tł'óógóó t'éí baa

naanish hwiiłhé, jiní. Tł'éé' njighá, jiní. Yidziihę́ęni bił nááhwiiską́, jiní. Naakits'áadah ajíínilgo nihoníyá, jiní. Yiik'áihyiin dideest'ą́ą'go níłch'i yę́ę hoł ch'íhoní'ą́, jiní. Hanideel'įį́', t'áadoo nik'ihool'įįhdą́ą' dah ńdiidááh nichó bich'į', hałní jiní. Hachó baa náánizhníchą́ą́', jiní. Hanideel'įį́', shiłní níłch'i biyázhí, jiní jiní. Ha'át'éego shį́į́ dooleeł, shichó. T'áá shá ntsíníkeesgi[20] diné daats'í[21] baa shidiní'aah, jiní jiní. Ha'át'éego lá dooleeł, ąą' sitsóí. T'áá la' doo kónishłe'jí da, ní jiní. Ákohgo shį́į́ éí i'íí'ą́.

[19]This should read: *doo hah adidit'aah da jiní*. As it stands *góó* and the following *wónáásdóó* are hard to combine.

[20]*T'áá shá ntsíníkeesgi*, whatever you have decided let that happen to me.

[21]Imperfect form, but *daats'í* gives it the sense of a future tense: "perhaps you will turn me over to them."

9. Ats'os bee bighaní

40. Hwiiłkáahgo, Díí hayíiłkąągo nihik'i dah adijeeh, hałní jiní, níłch'i biyázhí yęę. Kojí daats'í dah dideesháał, be'ek'id hóteel bibąąhjí. Kwe'é daats'í deesdzih nisin, jiní jiní. Ha'át'éego shįį shá baa ntsíníkees, bijiní jiní. Áko shįį díí tł'ée'go hachóhęę ch'é'etiingi ałts'ąąjí neezké. Éí shįį aadóó haídíl'įį'go yiską. Ńlááhdęę' hayíiłkąągo hachóhęę nááts'íílid haíńlá. T'áá áko be'ek'id hóteel bibąąhjį' dashdiiyá, jiní. Ńt'éé' dashdiiyáhąągóó hahodíídlááď, jiní, k'ad háajį' náhodoodleełgo biniiyé. Aadęę' shįį hakéédęę' diné deezhjéé' hodiyoolyééł biniiyé. Ałts'ąąjí íijéé', ła' hakéédęę', jiní. Aadęę' diné dahodeeskáá', be'ek'id hóteel bibąąhjį' adahaskáá'. Aadóó shįį nááts'íílid dzideedéél tákáá' bikáazhdeeyá. Ńléí táá'ałníi'di tł'oh dich'íízh dah shizhóód biyi' góne' ajííyá. Nááts'íílidęę' wóshdęę' kójiilaa. Ákóne' hakéé' ahootah, jiní. Tł'oh dich'ízhęę hayaagi ałnánizhnínil, bikáá' dasneezdá, jiní. Áko shįį t'áá ákóyah dzizdáago kodęę' diné hózníłteel. Tábąąhjį' t'áá ahakéé' ńt'ée'go aadóó ałts'ąąjį' ch'ééh ahéézníłteel. Ch'ééh ádaat'įįgo i'íí'ą, jiní. Háájí lá silįį' lá. Táłtł'ááh góyah daats'í silįį', dahałní jiní, éí t'óó azdiits'a'go.

41. I'íí'ąągo ałtso aná'iisdee', jiní. Áko índa nízhdii'na', jiní, tł'oh dich'ízhęę biyi'dęę'. Áádóó índa ndzizghal, ńt'éé' ádin, jiní. Ch'ééh hadzíisid, jiní. Aadóó nááts'íílid ha'naa ninázhníłdéél, jiní. K'ad bikáá'góó dah ńdiidááh, ałtso aná'iisdee', ńléidi t'óó naa yádaałti', hałní jiní, hajaat'ahdęę' níłch'i biyázhí yęę. Hachó baa ńdzídzá, jiní, tł'ée'go. Ha'át'íigi lá nihinídzíí', sitsóí shi'awéé', hałní jiní, Adinóól-gháázh lágo, sitsóí, áyaadąą' t'áá íniih, hałní jiní. Ch'é'etiingi ałts'áahjí neezké, jiní. Haa ályąągo t'áá ákǫǫ hwiiską, jiní.

42. Ńdiidááh, sitsóí. Hayíílkáą, hałní jiní. K'ad t'áá áajį' dah náádidíídááł. T'áá áajį' t'éí t'áá hasih, be'ek'id hóteeljį',[22] hałní jiní. Wóniijį' dah diiyá, jiní, ostsidii nilínę́ę. Ałtį́į' diłhił yit'įį́ lá, jiní. Atsee' beest'áán yit'įį́ lá, jiní. Hainílá, jiní. Díí k'ad be'ek'id hóteel bibąąhjį' dah náádidíídááł. Ákwii k'ai' bee nighan ádííłííł. Ákwii díí bee na'íłtseed doo, hałní jiní. Éí éí áajį' dah náázdiidzá. Ákwii k'ai' bee haghan ájiilaa, jiní. T'áá hwee kónishéíígo ch'ilátah hózhóón bee ajíshjéé', jiní.

43. Biyi'gi dzizdáá ńt'éé', da'níłts'ą́ą́'dę́ę́' hahodíídlááď, jiní. Ńt'éé' díí t'áá ch'é'etiindóó ńléí tábąąhgi ahénál'á silįį́', jiní, jádídlǫ́'ii. Aadóó toojį' dah deezhjéé', jiní. Ła' t'áá nahdę́ę́' deíjeeh, jiní. T'áá áko ałtį́į' diłhiłę́ę bił hajíídéél, atsee' beest'ánę́ę bił. Aajį' ła' dziskaa', jiní. Ła' bił hanáájídéél tsék'is diitsoii wolyéii ła' bee náádzískaah, jiní. Hats'ą́ąjį' náás kódzaa, jiní. Hak'a'ą́ą nízhdiinil, jííghánę́ę ałdǫ́' nízhdiinil. Haghan biyi'gi nizhnínil, jiní. Bíjíínizh, jiní. T'áá sitį́į ńt'éé' t'áá áła. Kohgo dah nályoł, jiní. Teeł daak'ání tábąąhgóó hólǫ́, jiní. Éí ła' jíínizh, jiní. T'áá hwee kóníłtsázígo hozdeezgeed, ákóyah teeł daak'ánę́ę nizhníłjéé'. Bikáa'gi ats'os nizhníłjéé'. Biyi' góyah dzineeztį́, jiní, i'íí'ą́ągo.

44. Ńlááhdę́ę́' hayíílką́ągo, Doo sonááhodéébéezh da ńlááhdę́ę́' k'ad diné nik'i dah náánájih, hałní jiní, hatł'aahdę́ę́' níłch'i biyázhí yę́ę. K'ad tł'oh dich'íízh biyi' góne' dah náádíídááh. Nááts'íílid ádił tánááníideeł, k'ad doo sonááhodéébéezh da, hałní jiní. Nááts'íílid yę́ę dzideezdéél, bikáa'jį' deeyá tł'oh dich'ízhę́ę biih náádzoodzá. Hakéédę́ę́' nááts'íílidę́ę ach'į' náájooldéél. Tł'oh dich'ízhę́ę ałná-ninááżhníłjoł bikáá' náázneezdá. Diné hó nááznííłteel. Kǫ́ǫ́ la' bighan ńt'éé' lá. Ats'os la' biyi' nábiiłkááh. Háájí lá silįį́' lá ats'os bee bighaní, ho'doo'niid jiní. Ch'ééh háká ánááhóót'įįd, ts'ídá ałtsogóó tábąąhgóó. Ch'ééh háká áhát'įįgo anáá'oot'ą́, jiní. Nááts'íílidę́ę bikáá' dah náádziidzį́, jiní, i'íí'ą́ągo. Haghanęęjį' ha'naa bikáá' ninááᴅzídzá, jiní. Ats'osę́ę biyi'góó nááhwiiską́, jiní.

45. Hayíílką́ągo, Ńdíídááh, hałní jiní, níłch'i biyázhí. Ha'a'aahjį' díní'įį́', ho'doo'niid jiní. Áajį' dzideezghal, ńt'éé' k'osishchíín[23]

[22]*-jį'*, toward is ordinarily low-nasal, but here being separated from *t'áá áajį'*, the tone is raised *-jí*, toward the lake he starts.

[23]The informant has forgotten to mention the color of clouds. So this sentence should read: *ńt'éé' k'os diłhił k'osishchííngo níłch'i diłhił.*

nizhónígo ałde dah sinil, jiní. Bikáádę́ę́' níłch'i dah sizį́, jiní. Shádi'ááhjį' náádígaał, ho'doo'niid jiní. Ń't'éé' k'os dootł'izh k'osishchíingo naaki ałde[24] dah sinil, jiní. Bikáádę́ę́' níłch'i dootł'izh dah náánásdzį́, jiní. E'e'aahjį' náádígaał, náho'doo'niid jiní. Ń't'éé' k'os łitso k'osishchíingo naaki ałk'i dah sinil, jiní. Bikáádę́ę́' níłch'i łitso dah náánásdzį́, jiní. Náhookǫsjį' náádígaał, ho'doo'niid jiní. Ń't'éé' k'os łigai k'osishchíingo naaki ałk'i dah sinil jiní. Bikáádę́ę́' níłch'i łigai dah náánásdzį́, jiní.

46. Ha'a'aahjí yę́ę áhální jiní, k'ad lá ha'át'íísh dó' daa dandoolííł. K'ad lá shiyázhí nílį ni, sitsói nílį ni, hałní jiní. Shádi'ááhjí yę́ę t'áá kónááho'doo'niid níłch'i dootł'izhę́ę. E'e'aahdę́ę́' níłch'i łitsooí yę́ę t'áá kónááho'doo'niid, jiní. Náhookǫsdę́ę́' níłch'i łigaií yę́ę t'áá kónááho'doo'niid, jiní. Aajį' atah ninстанhodeet'ą́. Nichó éí t'áá náhoo'áałii bik'ehgóó ánít'ée doo, hałní jiní, níłch'i diłhił. Índa éidí nihíndziihígíí biniinaa ánídil'íinii nił bééhózin, hałní jiní. T'áá nik'iidoot'ihgo át'é. Azhą́ ákót'ée ndi, sitsói, hałní jiní. Jó nił bééhózinii hólǫ́ nit'į́, hałní jiní. Azhą́ shį́į́ ákót'éego hojiniih ndi t'áá ałtso bikáá' dooleeł, hałní jiní.

[24] *Ałde*, not necessarily resting on each other, although this is evidently meant.

10. Yá'ąąshgi nááts'íílid hoł hahaazdéél

47. K'ad nichó bich'į' dah ńdidíídááł, hałní jiní. Aadę́ę́' yee nich'į' hanáánádzíihii béého̜zingo, éí bik'ehgo dah náádidíídááł, hałní jiní. Lą́'ąą k'ad ákǫ́ǫ́ dah ńdideeshdááł, jiní jiní. Áadi hachó sikéhę́ędi baa ńdzídzá, jiní. Nił béého̜zin shį́į́, sitsóí shi'awéé', hałní jiní. Ha'át'íí át'é nínízin, sitsóí, nił ch'íhoní'ánígíí, hałní jiní. K'os diłhił lá át'é ni. Níłch'i diłhił lá át'é ni. Éí lá shił hoolne' ni, jiní jiní. Ha'át'íí bíni' bik'ehgóó át'é nínízin, sitsóí, hałní jiní. Ni lá bidiní, ní jiní, níłch'i biyázhí hajáát'ahdę́ę́'. Nihí lá nihíni' bik'ehgo ni, sitsóí, bijiní jiní. T'áá lá aaníí ni, ní jiní. Éí íínít'įįdígíí t'áá nik'iidoot'ihgo át'é, sitsóí, hałní jiní, azhdííláhígíí ááhyiłní, jiní.

48. Hoos'įįdgò t'óó ha'ó'áłígo be'ek'id hóteel ałníí'jį' ńdíínááł, hałní jiní. Éí áájí nííníyáago nááts'íílid neheł'áahgi ałnánidííléél. Éí nił dah hididoodił, hałní jiní. Ńléí yá'ąąshgi nił hahidoodił. Éí nił hahaazdéelgo t'áá shį́į́ ńdiil'ashgo át'é, sitsóí, hałní jiní. Éí t'áá ákǫ́ǫ́ hwiiską́, jiní.

49. T'áá áko aadóó dashdiiyáhí tá'áłníí'jį' nizhníyá, jiní. Nááts'íílidę́ę hakéth'áahgi ahideełnáá nizhnílá, jiní. Ha'a'aahjígo tóhę́ę hideesnáá', jiní. Shádi'ááhjí ákónáánádzaago t'áá wódahgo hoł nihinídéél,[25] jiní. E'e'aahjí náhideesnáa'go ńléí bi'oh oonaah, t'áá wódahgo hoł nihinídéél, jiní. Náhookǫsjí t'áá ákónáánádzaago nízaagóó hoł nihinídéél, jiní. Nask'ol, jiní, ałníí'gi t'áá át'é.

50. Jó áko yághahóókáá' góne' hahodzizlįįd. Diné hólǫ́ǫ́ lá, jiní, ałdó' ááji. Hatáál lá, jiní. Tł'óogi n'dii'ááh,[26] jiní. N'dii'ááh.[27] Baa

[25] *Nihińdéél*, soft *h* not *nixińdéél.*

[26] Glottal stop after *n'* seems to require high tone on *n'*. Properly it is low toned *n'dii'ááh*. After sandpainting is completed the *ndii'ááh* are stuck around the sandpainting and are then called *inánees'ááh* "stuck in around."

[27] This should probably read: *ndii'ááh baa dahóóchįįd* uprights got angry with him (for intruding). (Sandoval.)

ná'oochiih, jiní. Iikááh baa na'aldeeh, jiní, yah ajííyáago. Ńléí hataałii bíighahdi hahoo'a', jiní. Tóee hatáál lá, jiní. Tééhołtsódí hastiin hataał lá, jiní. Ha'át'éédę́ę́' lá yínááł, sitsóí. Kohaniigi nihookáá' diné doo naagháa da, hałní jiní. T'áá ałtsogo naasháago át'é, jiní jiní. Tó názbąsdę́ę́' lá ásht'í ni. Be'ek'id hóteeldę́ę́' lá ásht'į ni, jiní jiní.

51. Iikááh baa na'aldeeh, jiní. Níłtsą́ ashkii yaa naa'eesh, jiní. Naal'eełí tsíłkéí, díí yaa naakai lá, jiní. Naal'eełí doo naat'a'ígíí tsíłkéí,[28] díí ałdó' lá, jiní. Tábąsdisí dó'[29] tsíłkéí, díí dó', jiní. Tábąsdisíłbáí tsíłkéí, díí dó'. Daak'įį' tsíłkéí, díí dó'. Yáá'azhjool tsíłkéí, díí dó'. Tooji noołna' tsíłkéí, díí dó'. Tooji ndiigai tsíłkéí, díí dó'. Tooji nahabił tsíłkéí, díí dó'. Hoz tsíłkéí, díí dó'. Dih tsíłkéí, díí dó'. Tó níłhę́shii tsíłkéí, díí dó'. Dééł dine'é tsíłkéí binant'a'í, díí dó'. Ii'ni' tsíłkéí, díí dó'. Díí shįį iikááh yaa naakai lá, jiní.

52. Aadóó shįį ch'ał hastiin díí yíníłkad yich'į' ał'áá' lá, jiní. Ch'ał nineezí tsíłkéí, wónaalch'ilii tsíłkéí, ts'ǫǫ sání tsíłkéí, chaa' tsíłkéí, tábąstíín tsíłkéí, tsisteeł tsíłkéí, ch'ééh digháahii tsíłkéí, tsilghááh tsíłkéí, tł'iish ánínígíí bitáá ńdzísgaiígi tsíłkéí, tótł'iish tsíłkéí, tł'iishk'aa' tsíłkéí binant'a'í, aajį' nineel'ą́. Aadóó bi'áadii ts'ídá ałtso bąąh náánííjaa'. Ákohgo shįį hanááł iikááh ninásdziid. Tł'ée'go hanááł ts'aa' yaa ninááánátą́. Jiníyáádóó táa'di hanááł ts'aa' yaa niitą́. Ákohgo bijį́. T'áá áko hanáałgo anáá'oot'ą́. Óhojiił'aahgo át'éé lá, jiní.

53. Ákohgo hachóhę́ę honíł'áázh, jiní. Da' shínooł'ázhísh ni, shichó, bijiní jiní. Aoo', sitsóí, níniil'áázh lá, hałní jiní. Ńláahgi dáádiníláii ályaa, jiní. Shádi'ááhjígo tł'iish ánínígíí bidíneesdá, jiní. Náánáłahjígo éí tótł'iish, jiní. Dootso diłhił ałch'į' adeez'áahgi hólǫ́ǫ́ lá, jiní. Hachóhę́ę yah íí'áázh, jiní. Shádi'ááhjígo bá hoo'a'. Sáanii nilįįgo bitsiiba' łigaigo ńléídę́ę́' bits'ą́ą́' dahozhdiilįįd yę́ę ch'ikéí násdlįį' lá, jiní. Tééhołtsódii hastiin bicheii lá, jiní. Bidinínáádę́ę́' bitsóóké lá, jiní. Kodóó níłtsą́ ashkii bitsóí lá, jiní. Bidinínáádę́ę́' bichó lá, jiní. Ákohgo kwe'é k'é béédahózin, jiní. Áadi índa at'éézniizį́į', jiní, t'áá ałtsogóó ats'os bee bighaní. Ákódzaa, jiní.

[28] Or *tsíłkééh*. Final *i* is faint.

[29] Or: *tábąsdísí*.

11. Shádíín ashkii

54. K'ad t'áá ha'ísíidgo yiidoołkááł, ho'doo'niid jiní. Dootso diłhił tééhołtsódii hastiin níłtsą́ ashkii yiłgo ání, jiní. Tééhołtsódii hastiinę́ę hanáánádzíí'. Dáádinílái nohłínígíí nihí dó' há'ohsíid dooleeł, hałní jiní. Níłtsą́ ashkii hanáánádzíí'. T'áá ákót'éego lá yá'át'ééh ni. T'áá há'ohsíid, hałní jiní áajį'. Lą́'ąą, jiní jiní, t'áá ájíła. Jó tooji hwiidzohdi bidahojííłįįd aadóó tó názbąsjį' áhojííłįįd índa be'ek'id hóteeljį' ákwii baa ałtah ńjídáahgo doo bił jílį́į da. Dich'ízhí dahodííniid. Nahodidáhí dahodííniid. T'áá woshch'ishgi ats'os yee bighaní ho'doo'niid. Jó k'ad kodi índa t'áá jilínę́ę t'áá házhi'ę́ę bee hodééjiih. Shádíín ashkii, ho'doo'niid. Díidí baa ádahołyą́ą dooleeł. Éí biniiyé háda'ídół'į́į', hałní jiní, tééhołtsódii hastiin.

55. Ii'ni' dine'é baa ayahoolniih, ní jiní. Binant'a'í nilíinii ii'ni' diłhił ha'a'aahjí dah sitíinii doo yá'áshǫ́ǫ da, ní jiní. Índa shádi'ááhjí ii'ni' dootł'izh binant'a'í nilíinii dah sitíinii doo yá'áshǫ́ǫ da, ní jiní. E'e'aahjí dah sitíinii ii'ni' łitso binant'a'í nilíinii doo yá'áshǫ́ǫ da, ní jiní. Náhookǫs biyaajį' ii'ni' łigai binant'a'í nilíinii doo yá'áshǫ́ǫ da, ní jiní. Índa níłch'i ntł'aaí doo yá'áshǫ́ǫ da, ní jiní. Níłch'i łikizhii doo yá'áshǫ́ǫ da, ní jiní. Ii'ni' ntł'aaí wolyéii, ii'ni' łikizhii wolyéii doo yá'áshǫ́ǫ da, ní jiní. Aajį' shį́į ákódzaago bee nahodínéestą́ągo ákǫ́ǫ naalchi'í ádahodiilyaa. Lą́'ąą, hada'ídiil'ínę́ę dooleeł, dazhdííniid.

56. Akohgo shį́į jóhonaa'éí bighandę́ę' tséghádińdínii ashiiké yíkai, jiní. Kodi t'áá hóoghahdi bá hoo'a', jiní. Tééhooltsódii hastiinę́ę ání jiní. Háádę́ę' lá ádaaht'į, sitsóóké, ní jiní. Jóhonaa'éí bighandę́ę' lá, ní jiní. Ákohgo shį́į díí dáádinílái nilínę́ę shádi'ááhjí nilíinii yoołgaii biyeel ályaa, jiní. Náhookǫsjí nilíinii tadzis'eełí biyeel ályaa, jiní.

Ha'át'íí biniiyé naahkai, sitsóí,[30] ní jiní. Jó azhą́ ákót'ée ndi ha'át'éegoshą' ła' t'áá ádin nahółá, hałní jiní. Ha'át'éegi, sitsóóké, jiní jiní.

57. Bich'áayah góne' adoolnii' aadę́ę́' náhálnih biyázhí wolyéii hayíílá, jiní. Jó díí hólǫǫgo t'éí tóee hojitaał dooleeł, jiní jiní. K'eet'áán yáłti'ii wolyé, jiní. K'ad índa bidziilgo nahodíítał, shicheii, hałní jiní. Ńléí wónii'góó ts'aa' bii' nléeh. Áko t'éí doo nits'ą́ą́' ninaádidoolyéeł da, ho'doo'niid jiní. K'ad bizhíyiizhish, ho'doo'niid jiní. Éí bik'ehgóó k'ad ákódeiit'į́, dahwiitaałii. K'adígíí baa naahkai ndi ła' diné doo deíniih da; doo dabíínáał da, ní jiní. Ha'át'éegi lá ła' diné naagháá shį́į́, doo yiniih da. Ałtsogo lá yínii' ni', jiní jiní. Doodago shį́į́ ádíní, hałní jiní. Díí k'ad niníłt'éehdi hái bee nidííłt'ih, ho'doo'niid jiní. Jó t'áadoo yit'íhígíí t'óó ndoot'ih. Ha'át'éegoshą' ádadohní, sitsóóké, jiní jiní.

58. Doodago shį́į́ ádíní. Ńléí naa ílyáígíí jóhonaa'éí nihaínílá. K'ad doo bił adoodzihgóó ńlááhgóó silá bił oodzii'góó. Doo nihozhńtáál yidoolyéeł da, ní jiní. Lą́'ąą, sitsóóké. Jó doo shił bééhózin da. Áko nidoołt'ihii háadi nihił béédahózingo ádadohní, sitsóí,[30] ní jiní. Nihił lá béédahózin nihí, ní jiní, tséghádińdínii ashiiké. Sisnaajiní bilátahgi hólóonii ayáásh dootł'izh dine'é tsíłkéí, díí lá ndadidoo'áał ni', ní jiní. Tsoodził bilátahgi tashchizh dootł'izh dine'é tsíłkéí, díí lá ndadidoo'áał ni', hayííłką́ągo, ní jiní. Dook'o'oosłííd ndadidoo'áał ni', ní jiní. Dibé ntsaa bilátahgi aniłt'ánii dine'é tsíłkéí, díí lá ndadidoo'áał ni', ní jiní. Kojį' ha'oodzíí, jiní, ałch'į' deez'áhíjį'. Weehee, dootso diłhił ahéénílyeed, ho'doo'niid jiní. Ajoolwod, jiní. T'áadoo dó' hodíína'í ńjílwod, jiní. Daashą' yit'é hayííłką́ągo shį́į́ dah diikah, dahodoo'niid, jiníigo ńjílwod. Lą́'ąą, jó kót'éé lá, jiní jiní, tééhooltsódii, níłtsą́ ashkii dó'.

[30]This should read: *sitsóóké*.

12. Tóee bijį́

59. T'áá shįį́ áko ts'aa' yaa niitą́, jiní. Bińjízhish, jiní, ts'ídá t'áá ájít'é. Doo tł'óo' njigháa da, ho'doo'niid jiní. Aadóó adideest'ą́ tééhoołtsódii atsáłee niidiní'ą́, jiní. Weehee, ni k'ad anilyeed, ho'doo'niid jiní. Ats'os yee bighaní nizhńjaa', jiní, ła' hayiin, naal'eełí ntsaaígíí tsíłkéí. Weehee, nihiyiin ła' ndanohjááh,[31] ho'doo'niid jiní. Nizhńjaa', jiní. Ákohgo hayiin yileeł. Naal'eełí doo naat'a'ígíí tsíłkéí biyiin ła' niiníjaa'. Tábąsdisítso biyiin ninéiníjaa'. Tábąsdisí áłts'íísígíí haa náádeet'ą́ hayiin ła' atah nináázhníjaa'. Tooji ndiigai tsíłkéí haa náádeet'ą́ hayiin ła' nináázhníjaa'. Tooji nahabił tsíłkéí haa náádeet'ą́ hayiin ła' atah ninááníjaa'. Hoz dine'é tsíłkéí hayiin ła' atah nináázhníjaa'. Tó nílhęshii tsíłkéí hayiin ła' atah nináázhníjaa'. Dih tsíłkéí hayiin ła' atah nináázhníjaa'. Dééł dine'é tsíłkéí hayiin ła' atah nináázhníjaa', naat'agi yęę ałtso.

60. Kodóó shádi'ááhdóó táłtł'ááh náhálgai hoolyéédę́ę́' dine'é, dził tánííʼ silá hoolyéédę́ę́', dził tánííʼ naazlá hoolyéédę́ę́' ch'ał hastiin haa deet'ą́. Hágoshįį́ niyiin ła' atah ninííjááh, ho'doo'niid jiní. Ła' nizhníjaa'. Ch'ał nineezí tsíłkéí, Tį', náho'doo'niid. Tádzís'eełí hoolyéédóó ts'ǫǫs sání tsíłkéí biyiin ła' atah ninéiníjaa'. Tádílkǫǫhí hoolyéédóó ts'ǫǫs sání tsíłkéí biyiin ła' atah ninéiníjaa'. Niní'áídóó chaa' tsíłkéí biyiin ła' atah ninéiníjaa'. Táłtł'ááh náhálgaidóó tábąstíín tsíłkéí baa náádeet'ą́, biyiin atah ninéiníjaa'. Táłtł'ááh náhálgaidóó tsisteeł tsíłkéí baa náádeet'ą́. Táłtł'ááh náhálgaidóó ch'ééh digháahii tsíłkéí biyiin ła' atah ninéiníjaa'. Tó názbąsdóó tsiligháán tsíłkéí biyiin

[31] *Já*, refers to the set of songs.

łaʼ atah ninéiníjaaʼ. Beʼekʼid hóleelí hoolyéédóó tótłʼiish tsíłkéí baa náádeetʼą. Dego hołkʼááʼ[32] hoolyéédóó tłʼiishkʼaaʼ tsíłkéí baa náádeetʼą.

61. Hayííłką, jiní. Hayoołkááł bikʼijįʼ yéʼii bicheii ádííniid jiní, Tʼah wóshchʼishídę́ęʼ ánáádooʼniid. Tʼah wóshchʼishídę́ęʼ ánáádooʼniid. Áko táaʼdi ádííniid. Chʼéʼetiindę́ęʼ ánáádooʼniid. Ákohgo dį́įʼdi ádííniid. Yah íiyá bikéédę́ę́ʼ hashchʼéoghan yah íiyá. Doo sidasiłniiʼ da ndi níyá, ní jiní. Shí ałdóʼ doo sidasoołniiʼ da ndi níyá, ní jiní hashchʼéoghan. Shiyiin łaʼ atah dooleeł, sizééʼ nahontłʼah, ní jiní hashchʼééłtiʼí. Hashchʼéoghan tʼáá ákónáádooʼniid, jiní, biyiin łaʼ atah niidiníʼą, jiní. Ayáásh dootłʼizh yę́ę aadę́ęʼ łaʼ nináánálwod, jiní. Łaʼ ninéidiníʼą, jiní, tłʼóódę́ęʼ shį́į ałkééʼ niiʼihíʼnilgo. Tashchizh dootłʼizh tsíłkéí[33] yah anáánálwod, jiní. Łaʼ[34] ninéidiníʼą, jiní. Choozhghálii tsíłkéí yah annáánálwod jiní. Łaʼ ninéidiníʼą, jiní. Aniłtʼánii tsíłkéí yah anáánálwod, jiní. Łaʼ ninéidiníʼą, jiní. Aajįʼ ałtso jiní.

62. Tééhołtsódii hastiinę́ę akweʼé bihózhǫ́ǫjí niidiníʼą, jiní. Kʼad lą́ táidoołdaah niʼ, danihighangóó táidoołdaah, ní jiní. Aajįʼ, jiní. Atsʼos yee bighaní yę́ę tʼéí tʼáá ákǫ́ǫ naaghá, jiní. Hachó dóʼ tʼáá áła tʼáá ákǫ́ǫ, jiní.

[32] *Dego hołkʼááʼ* (water) place in sky. The place is mythical.

[33] *Tsíłkéí* or *tsíłkéé* here and in the following, the informant is not particular about pluralizing the predicate. The singular form *tsíłkę́ęh* could be substituted to correspond with the predicates.

[34] *Łaʼ* may refer to "one set" or "some" songs.

13. Kin nteeldi doo bi'deeldlaadí

63. Hachó bich'į' hadzoodzíí', jiní. Shichó, háadi lá kin nteel hoolyé, jiní jiní. Nchxǫ', doo ájíníí da, Bik'ijį'[35] hóyéé' haz'ą́, hałní jiní. Ha'át'íishą' hólǫ́ǫgo niniih, sitsóí, hałní jiní. Jó doo bi'deedlaad bich'į' deesháál, Nchxǫ', sitsóí, bik'ijį' hóyéé' haz'ą́. T'áá ałtsooí baa ńchį', hałní jiní. Áko lá t'áá ákǫ́ǫ deesháał ni', shichó, bijiní jiní. Tooji hwiidzohdę́ę́' tsíłkéí hát'į ni,[36] daaníi doo. Áłtsé áhodiilzééh, hałní jiní. Shí lá k'ad ákǫ́ǫ ńdeeshdááł ni'. Nánísdzáagoó ni[37] ha'át'éego dooleeł, hałní jiní, tooji hwiidzoh asdzą́ą́.

64. Náátsʼíilidę́ę áayah niídeel, jiní. Yik'i haayáádóó bił áhootah jineesk'olígíí áhoodzaa, jiní. Bi'áłchíní yę́ę ałníí' neezdá, jiní. Áadi, áadi, éí hoshdódii bidááh diníláá lá, jiní. Tooji hwiidzoh bihádídíín áyiilaa lá. Azee' bíni'ii bihádídíín ánááyiidlaa lá, jiní. Azee' yidlohii bihádídíín ánááyiidlaa lá, jiní. Kétsįh haachíí' shílátsoh wolyé, t'áá éí bihádídíín ánááyiidlaa lá, jiní. Áko dįį' bihádídíín ályaa, jiní.

65. K'ad tsíłkéí yah adoojah, t'áálá́hídi bich'į' haasdzíí', ní jiní. Dibénii'í tsíłkéí ajiłee haniihgo ni'éé' bee adíílwoł. Zahalánii tsíłkéí ajiłee haniihgo ni'éé' bee adíílwoł. Tsé noolch'óshiiłbáhí ni dó' ni'éé' bee adíílwoł. Tsé noolch'óshiiłchíí' tsíłkéí ni'éé' bee adíílwoł índa nidloh dó'. Tsįįłkaałii tsíłkéí ni dó' ni'éé' bee adíílwoł ajiłee haniihgo. Tsin yąąh dzootihí tsíłkéí ni dó' ni'éé' bee adíílwoł. Ni éí ts'ídá alátahgi

[35]That is, the place is full of risks. *Hóyéé'* place-risk, *haz'ą́* there is a particular place, *bik'ijį'* on that place.

[36]Instead of: *Ha'át'íí nee'*, what we'll see. Final *e* is often omitted.

[37]Instead of: *nánísdzáagoónee'*.

doo bi'deedlaad yił yah íiyáadi ni'éé'ígíí bee adíílwol, bi'doo'niid jiní, k'aalógiitsoh. Ni anił'ání nilínígíí ni áadi ni'éé'ígíí bee adíílwoł índa nizhííhígíí ádíníigo, ho'doo'niid jiní. Kót'ée ho'doo'niid. Lá'ąą, dazhdííniid.

66. Aadóó nááts'íílidę́ę yikáá' hanásdzá bił anáhootah. Hatsóí yę́ę baa ńdzídzá, jiní, áadi. Díí tooji hwiidzoh bihádídíín, azee' bíni'í bihádídíín, azee' yidlohii bihádídíín índa kétsį́h haalchíí' bihádídíín, ákohgo dį́į' bihádídíín bitsóí yę́ę yeiníláá lá, jiní. Doo sohodoobéezhii bich'į' hodíníłchį́, sitsóí, hałní jiní. Áadi bił yah ííníyáago k'aalógiitsoh biih dííłwod bikáagi dį́į'di ałk'iidíít'aahgo bitahgi díníidaał na'akáąhgo sikéego. K'ad kót'é jó ákon, sitsóí. Nihí éí díí k'ad t'ą́ą' dah ńdidiit'ash tooji hwiidzohjį', t'áá ákǫ́ǫ honiidlǫ́ǫ doo, ní jiní. Díí k'adígíí tóee ajiłee bił ahihodit'ih wolyéédóó ahą́ąh dijih, ní jiní. Kojí tóee ńt'i' doo, ní jiní Łahjí ajiłee bihózhǫ́ǫjí ńt'i' doo, ní jiní. Ńláh k'ad, sitsóí, dah diinááh. Nihí ałdó' k'ad t'ą́ą' dah ńdidiit'ash háádiń[36] ałk'éé dahodiidleeł, ní jiní.

67. Hachóhę́ę dah ńdiit'áázh, jiní. T'áá shį́į áko dibénii'í jílwod. Shi'éé' biih nilyeed, sitsóí, jiní jiní. Diné t'óó ahayóí, jiní áko. Aadóó shį́į ńláahgóó bee tazhdít'ááh, ájíníigo ła' ayóigi dah náázhnídaahgo. Díí diné ałníí' njigháhą́ą ádaaní jiní, Háájí lá ats'os yee bighaní íiyá. Kojį' la', t'áálahígo bideekéé', daaní jiní. Ńléiga' t'éí ńláahgóó tádílyeed, t'óó nizhónígo áníigo ndi, éísh éí át'į́į doo, dajiní jiní. Zahalánii yę́ę bi'éé' biih náájoolwod, yílk'idgo nahoní'ą́ądóó, jiní, yázhdíłtihgo. Ła' ayóigi dah názhńdaah, jiní, náánjoot'aahgo. Ńt'éé' kǫ́ǫ tsé noolch'óshii tsé yikáágóó dah na'alzhish, jiní. Bi'éé'ę́ę hach'į' ayííyį́, jiní. Aadóó éí bee nízaah ninááadzídzá. Ńt'éé' tsé noolch'óshiiłchíí' tsé yikáádóó anádloh, jiní. Dah nináá'álzhish, jiní.

68. Aadóó shį́į éí bee náás náázdeesdzá, ńléí tsé dańt'i'góó, bikáá náás joolwołgo. Ádin doo yaa áháyą́ą da, jiní. Áko éé'ę́ę t'óó hach'į' áńjii'nííł, jiní. T'ahaa joolwoł, ńt'éé' kǫ́ǫ tsį́įłkaałii ninááajiidá, jiní. Ha'éé'ę́ę haa náájígį́, jiní. Kǫ́ǫ, sitsóí, shi'éé' biih náánídááh, jiní jiní. Aadóó ńléí tsin dah naazhjaa'góó bee joolwoł, jiní. Ła' ayói tsin bińdajiłtązh, áhozhdil'į́įhgo. T'óó náájoolwoł. Ńt'éé' kǫ́ǫ tsįyąąh dzoot'íhí ninááajídááh. Kǫ́ǫ shi'éé', sitsóí, jiní jiní. Aadóó t'óó tsin bąąh hizhdilyeedgo bich'į' joolwoł, jiní. T'áá áyídígo si'ą́, jiní, kin nteel. Wónáásdóó biyaa ajoolwod, jiní. K'aalógiitsohę́ę biih náájoolwod, jiní. Ńléidi hachó tádídíín haińjaa'ą́ą t'áá ałtso hat'ah bikáágóó bił nááshdeezhchid. Ádąąh ájiilaa, jiní. Bił yah ájoot'a', jiní. Tséghádińdínii dah si'ą́ą́ lá, jiní.

69. Áko ałní'ní'ą́, jiní. Doo bik'i'diidlaad da lá. T'áá bi'ohídóó adiididlaad lá, jiní. Wóniijį'go sikéé lá, jiní. Wóniijį'go bitéelgo na'akąąhgo sikéé lá, jiní. Bikáagi dį́į'di ałk'ijiit'ahgo bik'ijį' azhdoogáád tádídíín hat'ah bąąh ájiilaaą́ą bik'ijį' nazhnííłdee', jiní. Nábítł'ahjígo iiłtsą́, jiní. Adińdíínę́ęgi hachaha'oh hodeeshzhiizhgo t'áá hakéé' ahéénághal, jiní bitahgizneezdá, jiní, ałts'ą́ąjį' sikéego. Hat'ah dzideesbaal, jiní, biyaajį'. Ostsidii nilínę́ę ání jiní, Yáadi lá nizhóní dó', shádí, bik'ehgo ńdiikąął, ní jiní. Bideezhí yę́ę shádí yidííniid, jiní. Ha'át'íí lá diní, shádí, ní jiní, akéédę́ę' nilínę́ę. Nideezhí yee' nishłį́, ní jiní. Bił ndiidił bik'ehgo ńdiikąął, shádí, jiní jiní. Ostsidii jílínę́ę hadeezhí yę́ę, shádí, bijiní jiní, hohoníyáago.

70. Nchxǫ', shádí, bíighahígi ádaat'é. Nchxǫ', nihiłní, jiní jiní. Áko lá t'áá bił ndiidił ni', shádí, jiní jiní. Ostsidii jílínę́ę. Áko lá t'óó nchógi át'éego k'é shidiní, jiní jiní. T'óó hat'áhąą nízhdííłbał, jiní, bitahgi ałch'ishdę́ę' honííł'į́igo. Wónáásdóó shį́į́ ałch'ishjí bíhoníyá. Ostsidii nilínę́ę aadę́ę' hak'idiilchidę́ę' bílágiizhdę́ę' haa joolwod, jiní. Akéédę́ę' nilínę́ę hak'idiilchidę́ę bílágiizhdę́ę' haa náájoolwod, jiní. Aadóó jidineez'aah díí hí'nii'ááhę́ęjį' yoołgaii hínii'áahgo. T'áá éí dį́į'go naa dah sitą́ągo ostsidii nilínę́ę ch'ééh hak'idiilchíidgo bílágiizhdę́ę' háájílwo'go, índa akéédę́ę' nilínę́ędóó t'áá ákót'éego. Wónáasii ła' naa dah sitą́ bikáajį' hazneez'aah.

71. Aadóó shį́į́ yoołgaii naaki naa dah sitą́ bikáajį' hazneez'aah. Yoołgaii táá' dah sitą́ bikáajį' kojį' hanáázneez'aah. Yoołgaii dį́į' dah sitą́ bikáajį' hanáázneez'aah. Ostsidii nilínę́ę ání jiní, Doo lá kojį' nihá haz'ą́ ńt'éé' ni', shádí, ní jiní, bideezhí yę́ę ááhyiłní jiní. Ch'ééh lá dooda nisin, ch'ééh doo shił aaníi da, ní jiní, akę́ędę́ę' nilínę́ę. Ch'ééh náás jidíní'ááh, jiní. Bich'į' t'ą́ą' ninááájiilyeedgo bił ashja'jił'į́igo nihá tsizhdíní'ááh, jiní.

72. Náásgóó bił náázdeeskai, jiní. Dá'ák'eh hóteel ałníijį' doo dó'ash ádzaa da, jiní, ałts'ą́ájí naayízí sikaadgo bitahgóó. Ńt'éé' ákǫ́ǫ naayízí náánáskaad, jiní. T'áá bí t'éí nahí ahaa naat'aashgo aniłt'ánii éé'ęę biih náájoolwod, jiní. Táá'iitsóhii yę́ę biih joolwod, jiní. Hoł ałch'į' ánádzaa, jiní. Lóó'óó, yiits'a'go ázhdííniid, jiní. Aajį' ha'a'aahdę́ę'go bich'į' nizhní'áázh. Koji la' ání, shádí, jiní jiní. Hadeezhí yę́ę ááłjiní jiní. Jó ákon nizhónígo ání, jiní jiní. Shádi'ááhdę́ę' bich'į' ninááájít'áázh, jiní. Háaji lá ání, jiní jiní. E'e'aahdę́ę' bich'į' ninááájít'áázh, jiní. T'áá kojį' ání, nizhónígo dó' ání, jiní jiní. Náhookǫsdę́ę'go bich'į' ninááájít'áázh, jiní. Háaji lá ání, bikétł'óólji'ísh bit'ą́ą' biyaaji'ísh, jiní jiní.

73. Táá'iitsohii yę́ę biyi'dę́ę' nízhdii'na', jiní, t'áá dinégo. Ostsidii nilínę́ę nishtł'ahjí hach'áayah ajííłt'e', jiní. Akéédę́ę' nilínę́ę nish'nááji ajííłt'e', jiní. Ałch'ishjí bizéé' jízhchid, jiní. Áko lá át'é dishní ni, shádí, ní jiní akéédę́ę' nilínę́ę. Éí índa t'áá aaníigi k'é, ní jiní. K'ad lá shį́į́' soolį́į' ni, bizhdííniid jiní. Akéédę́ę' nilínę́ę ání jiní. Áyąądą́ą' nihookáá' diné wolyéii t'áá ałtsogo haniih. Ákwe'é éí shį́į t'áá aaníí bee nihich'ą́ąh sínízį́įgo hool'áa doo, hałní jiní. T'áá áko ch'ilátah hózhǫ́nę́ę dajííłdlááad, jiní t'áá ádzíłtso. Bee ńdazniłtsxizgo[38] bee ooyą́ baa ndziskai, jiní. Aadóó hach'áayah ajíínilii bił nahajíkai, jiní, ha'a'aahjígo dibé ntsaa bich'į'. Ooyą́ baa jookahgo nízaad njíkai, jiní. Atsijį' njí'nil, jiní. Tį', bijiníigo hatsijį' deezh'áázh, jiní.

[38]This should read: *bee ńda'ahizniltsxisgo*.

14. Ii'ni' hastiin

74. Akéédę́ę́' t'įįhígo hizhdeezhtłizhígi nitł'ají bee hazhdooltáál, jiní, t'áá biłgo, shshd, hojiní jiní. T'áá dasdool'isgo dzizį́, jiní. Ch'ééh ndzizghal, jiní. Nish'nááji bee hanáázhdooltáál, jiní. T'áá kónááhozhdoo'niid, jiní. Ch'ééh ninááłdzísghal, jiní. Nishtł'ají bee hanáázhdooltáál, jiní. Shshd, nááhozhdoo'niid, jiní. Ch'ééh ninááłdzisghal, jiní. Nish'nááji bee hanáázhdooltáál, jiní. Shshd, nááhozhdoo'niid jiní. Ńt'éé' nahasdzáán biyi'dę́ę́' hajiiyííłtį, jiní. Ła', Hágo yéé, sitsóí, hałní jiní. Áajį' dashdiiyá, jiní. Ńt'éé' kóhoníłtsázígo ahóót'i', jiní. Ha'át'íí lá áhodiiyootsází góyah ajoogááł, shicheii, bijiní jiní. Hótsaago át'é, sitsóí, níinii yisoł jiní. Ńt'éé' kohgo áhoodzą́, jiní. Ńt'éé' kodę́ę́' ha'az'ą́, jiní. Dį́į'go ałde dah aztą́ą́ lá, jiní.

75. Ákóyah ajííyá, jiní, aajį'. Na'ashǫ́'ii dich'ízhii hastiin bighan lá, jiní. Áyói át'éii baa ńsíní'įįd, sitsóí, hałní jiní. Da' ntł'iz nit'į, hałní jiní. Yisht'į́į lá, bijiní jiní. Da' yoołgaii hólǫ́, hałní jiní. Hólǫ́ǫ́ lá, bijiní jiní. Da' dootł'izhii hólǫ́. Hólǫ́ǫ́ lá, bizhdííniid jiní. Da' diichiłí hólǫ́. Hólǫ́ǫ́ lá, bizhdííniid jiní. Da' bááshzhinii hólǫ́. Hólǫ́ǫ́ lá, bizhdííniid jiní. Jó t'áá ałtso hólǫ́ǫ́ lá, sitsóí, hałní jiní. Diné doo jooba'í át'é, sitsóí. Ndi shí hak'eh dishdlį́, hałní jiní. Shí lá éí shiiyeeldoon ntł'izígíí yoołkááłgóó, ní jiní. Kǫ́ǫ́ lá bee hak'eh adidlíinii hólǫ́ ni, ní jiní. Hooghan wóniijį' dah diiyá, jiní. Béésh diłhił hayíílá, jiní. Dį́į'di azlį́į'go áza'dííłkał, hałní jiní. Bee díiyoł dego wódahgo didíínił, hałní jiní. Łą́'ąą, shicheii, k'ad nihinááłdeeshdááł ni,[39] bizhdííniid jiní, haíńláago.

[39]*Lá--ni,* I can go now, since I have something to protect me.

76. Aadę́ę́' shį́į́ háádzísdzá ch'ikéí íí'ázhę́ęgóó dashdiiyá bikéé'. Náádeelk'id, jiní, áłts'íísígo haná'ą́ íí'áazh ni, jiní. Ńt'éé' ákǫ́ǫ́ siké, jiní. Ch'ilátah hózhóón yiyíinizh léi' yee naané, jiní. Ostsidii nilínę́ę, ání jiní, Yoó, háájí lá naninää ńt'éé', ní jiní. T'áá nahí sédáá ńt'éé', bijiní jiní. Aadóó ooyą́ baa náázdeeskai, jiní, dah hijí'niiłgo. Tó naagaijį' ni'íildee', jiní. Hak'igi k'os dah hists'id jiní. Ąą dashideeshgizh, jiní, t'áá ákódígi. Ostsidii nilínę́ę hanáánáádzíí', jiní. Áyąądą́ą́'[40] nihookáá' diné wolyéii haniih ha'ní. Áyąądą́ą́' t'áá awołí bee ánt'į, hałníinii hazénázhchid, jiní. Lą́'ąą, bizhdííniid jiní.

77. Nihidaałhęęsh silį́į́', jiní. Díí hanaagóó łedoolch'il, jiní. Ha'a'aahjígo łeezh hajíísi', jiní. Akóh, hałní jiní, nílch'i biyázhí yę́ę. Yódahgo nílį, bijiní jiní. Akóh nínáńtááh, hałní jiní, nílch'i biyázhí yę́ę. Shádi'ááhjí łenáádoolch'il; łeezh hanáájíísi', jiní. Bináázdeesol. Wódahgo nílį, bijiní jiní. Akóh nínáńtá, ní jiní nílch'i biyázhí. E'e'aahjí łenáádoolch'il, łeezh hanáádzíisi', jiní. P'ááh wódahgo nílį, bijiní jiní. Bináázdeessol, jiní. Akóh nínánítááh, jiní jiní, nílch'i biyázhí. Náhookǫsjí łenáádooch'il; łeezh hanáádzíisi', jiní. P'ááh wódahgo nílį, náábizhdoo'niid jiní. Nílch'i biyázhí yę́ę hanáádzoodzíí', jiní. Akóh ntsiit'áá' góne'. K'ad béésh diłhił ázaniłkaad beedíiyoł, hojiní jiní.

78. Náádeeshch'iłę́ę t'áá ńléí wódahgo nąąh dah yizdéél, jiní. Béésh diłhiłę́ę beezhdeeyol. Yiii, yiists'ą́ą́' ahosoolts'ą́ą́', jiní. Yiii, yiists'ą́ą́' anáhosoolts'ą́ą́' shádi'ááhjígo. Yiii, yiists'ą́ą́' ahosoolts'ą́ą́' e'e'aahjigo. Yiii, yiists'ą́ą́' anááhosoolts'ą́ą́' náhookǫsjígo. Áajį' bíighah azlį́į́', jiní. T'áá aaníí hóniih lá, hałní jiní, akéédę́ę́' nilínę́ę.

[40]The two *áyąądą́ą́'* have the sense: Since it is a known fact (that, as the saying goes, Earth People know all things), be sure you (do it with all your might).

15. K'eet'áán bídadiiyeelnááh

79. Náás dah náádiildee', jiní. Hadáahgi diné naajeeh, jiní. Ńt'éé' dólii t'éí naajeeh, jiní dinégo naajeehę́ę. T'į́įhígo ninááádazneesk'oł, ńt'éé' t'áá dinégo ninááńájeeh, jiní. Bich'į' ni'ííldee', jiní. Kohaniigi nihookáá' diné doo naagháa da. Ha'át'éédę́ę' lá wohkah, ní jiní ła'. Nihíshą' éí háádę́ę' ádaoht'į, bijiní jiní. Dóliidzilídę́ę' lá ádeiit'į ni, ní jiní. Da' dootł'izhii hólǫ́, ní jiní. Hólǫ́ǫ́ lá, bijiní jiní. Da' yoołgaii hólǫ́. Hólǫ́ǫ́ lá, bizhdííniid jiní. Éí lá danihiyeel doo ni, bideená nił ch'íhodeesh'ááł. hałní jiní. Yíní wolyéí ntsáhákees wolyéí haińlá, jiní. Díí bik'ehgo wohkah doo, hałní jiní, Díí dine'é ninániieel'ą́ąjį', ts'ídá áłtso biyeel álnííłii[41] bída hideelnáah doo, ní jiní. Éí bee bééhózin doo, ní jiní. Éí bik'ehgo bik'eet'ą' bídadiiyeelnááh. Lą́'ąą, kót'éé lá. K'ad nihinááádiikah, jiní jiní.

[41]Imperfect form. Future tense.

16. Ch'ał hastiin

80. Náás náádeesdee', jiní, níhwííłbįįhí bich'į'. Ńt'éé' hadááhgi nááts'íílid agodí anáánáát'i' éiyee'.[42] Ha'át'éego lá, dzinízin jiní, aajį' bich'į' jookahgo. T'áá áyídídę́ę bich'į' ńjíkai. Ńt'éé' naadą́ą' hólǫ́, jiní. Ńt'éé' ákwe'é ła' ndziiltsaadgo hojoogoł, jiní. Naabéhígodí wolyéii bee hojoogoł, jiní, ízdoosohgo. Bich'į' ńjíkaigo t'áá hoogołí hoogoł, jiní. Doo haińt'įį da, jiní. Kodóó dóó bich'į' hadzidziih da, jiní. T'óó baa ntsízníkéez, jiní. Ha'át'íí lá hastiin bikee' la' ayóí áníłnéézgo dó' hoogoł, dziniizį́į' jiní. Aoo', sitsói, áko lá ánísht'é ni. Shikee' lá ayóí áníłnééz, hałní jiní. Bídę́ę' haadzíí', jiní.

81. Hó dóó baa tsínáázníkéez. Ha'át'íí lá hastiin bijáád ayóí dó' áníłnéezgo hoogoł, dziniizį́į' jiní. Bídę́ę' hanáánádzíí'. Aoo', sitsói, áko lá ánísht'é ni. Shijáád lá ayóí áníłnéezgo hweeshgoł ni', ní jiní. Baa tsínáázníkéez. Ha'át'íí lá hastiin bitł'aahą́ą la' ádingo hoogoł, dziniizį́į' jiní. Aoo'éí, sitsói, áko lá ánísht'é ni. Shitł'áá lá ádingo hweeshgoł ni', ní jiní. Baa tsínáázníkéez. Ha'át'íí lá hastiin la' bíígháán adiyooshéíígo hoogoł, néizniidzį́į' jiní. Aoo'éí, sitsói, áko lá ánísht'é ni. Shííghaán lá kónísheíigo hweeshgoł ni', ní jiní. Baa tsínááníkéez, jiní. Hastiin la' bikáá' t'óó dich'íizhgo hoogoł, néizniidzį́į' jiní. Aoo'éí, sitsói. Shikáá' lá dich'íizhgo hweeshgoł, náádí'ní jiní. Baa tsínáázníkéez, jiní. Hastiin la' bitsiits'iin t'óó kóníłtéelgo bináá' la' hadoolkǫhgo hoogoł, néizniidzį́į' jiní. Aoo'éí, sitsói, sitsiits'iin lá kóníłtéelgo shináá' hadoolkǫhgo hweeshgoł ni', hałní jiní.

[42] Lengthened *éíyee'* is equivalent to "giving them the hint," or "for some unknown reason."

82. Baa tsínáázníkéez, jiní. Hastiin la' biyaayáh dah na'asolgo hoogoł, néizniidzį́į' jiní. Aoo'éí, sitsóí, shiyaayá lá dah naasolgo hweeshgoł ni, nááhodi'ní jiní. Baa tsínáázníkéez, jiní. Hastiin la' bizéé' t'óó kóhoníłtéelgo hoogoł, néizniidzį́į' jiní. Aoo'éí, sitsóí, shizéé' lá kóhoníłtéelgo hweeshgoł ni, hałní jiní. Kohaniigi nihookáá' diné doo naagháa da, sitsóí, hałní jiní. Shíká adíílwołgo, éí lá biniiyé ásht'į ni, shicheii, bijiní jiní. Ha'át'éegi níká adeeshwoł, sitsóí, hałní jiní. Níhwííłbįįhí bich'į' déyá. Ákwe'é shá baa ntsídíikos, shicheii, bijiní jiní.

83. Da' áko yoołgaii nit'į, hałní jiní. Hólǫǫ́ lá, shicheii, bijiní jiní. Da' áko dootłizhii hólǫ́, hałní jiní. Hólǫǫ́ lá, shicheii, bijiní jiní. Da' áko tádzís'ełí hólǫ́, hałní jiní. Hólǫǫ́ lá, shicheii, bijiní jiní. Haah, ní jiní. Da' nát'oh nit'į. Shá dįįh díílééł, hałní jiní. Yisht'į́į lá, shicheii, bijiní jiní. Da' áko ni ałdó' nát'oh nit'į. Shá dįįh díílééł, shicheii, bijiní jiní. Hólǫǫ́ lá, sitsóí, hałní jiní. Da' ninát'ozis hólǫ́, sitsóí, hałní jiní. Da' ni ałdó' ninát'ozis hólǫ́, shicheii, bijiní jiní. Hólǫǫ́ lá, sitsóí, bijiní jiní. Da' jóhonaa'éí bikáá' si'ą́, hałní jiní. Da' ni ałdó' jóhonaa'éí bikáá' si'ą́, shicheii, bijiní jiní. Da' tł'éhonaa'éí dó' bikáá' si'ą́, sitsóí, hałní jiní. Áko lá át'é ni, shicheii, bijiní jiní. Da' ni ałdó' tł'éhonaa'éí bikáá' si'ą́, shicheii, bijiní jiní. Áko lá át'e ni, sitsóí, hałní jiní.

84. Da' nát'oh biih náájiihii hólǫ́, sitsóí, hałní jiní. Hólǫǫ́ lá, shicheii, bijiní jiní. Da' ni ałdó' biih náájiihii hólǫ́, shicheii, bijiní jiní. Hólǫǫ́ lá, sitsóí, hałní jiní. Da' bee ńdiiltłi'ii hólǫ́, sitsóí, hałní jiní. Hólǫǫ́ lá, shicheii, bijiní jiní. Da' ni ałdó' bee ńdiiltłi'ii hólǫ́, shicheii, bijiní jiní. Hólǫǫ́ lá, sitsóí, hałní jiní. Haah, náádoo'niid jiní. Haníłtsóós, sitsóí, kóníłtsóós, hałní jiní. Hadzííłtsoozii kǫ́ǫ́ nizníłtsooz, jiní. Ni dó' haníłtsóós, shicheii, bijiní jiní. Hayííłtsoozii kǫ́ǫ́ niníłtsooz, jiní. Néidiinil, jiní. Jóhonaa'éídę́ę́' yinééł'į́į', ahąąh nininil, jiní. Łahdę́ę́' nínááyiiznil, jiní. Tł'éhonaa'éí bikáá' sinildę́ę́' yinééł'į́į', jiní. Nát'ostse' haní'aah, sitsóí, hałní jiní. Hajíí'ą́, jiní. Ni dó' haní'aah, shicheii, bijiní jiní. Hayíí'ą́, jiní.

85. Ha'át'íí át'é, sitsóí, nát'ostse'ígíí, hałní jiní. Dootł'izhii nát'ostse'í át'é, jiní jiní. Ha'át'íí bee naashch'ąą', sitsóí, hałní jiní. Yoołgaii bee naashch'ąą' ni, shicheii, bijiní jiní. Ni'éí, éí ha'át'íí át'é, bijiní jiní. Dootł'izhii nát'ostse' át'é, sitsóí, hałní jiní. Bikáagiígíí ha'át'íí át'é, bijiní jiní. Yoołgaii lá bee naashch'ąą' ni, sitsóí, hałní jiní. Hái bee ńdiiłtłi', sitsóí, hałní jiní. Tséghádińdínii hajíí'ąą ni, bikáá' dah dziz'ą́, jiní. Ni éí hái bee ńdiiłtłi', bijiní jiní. Tséghádińdínii hayíí'ąą ni yikáá' dah yiz'ą́, jiní. Haah, ní jiní.

86. Ńdiilwod, jiní. Adeesk'ą́ą́z, jiní. Naazghal, jiní. Hó dó' nízhdiilwod. Azdeesk'ą́ą́z, jiní. Ndzizghal, jiní. Hach'į' dah diiyáii hajéígií kóyiilaa, yidéesnii'go hodíína', jiní. Haah, ní jiní. Bich'į' dashdiiyá, jiní. Bijéígií kójiilaa, bizdéesnii'go hodíína', jiní. Áníhę́ęgi ázhdííniid, Haah, jidííniid jiní. Hawodgi néineezkaad, jiní. T'áá aaníí sitsói nílį́į́ lá, hałní jiní. Biwodgi názneezkaad, jiní. T'áá aaníí shicheii nílį́į́ lá, bijiní jiní. Hó dóó átsé hanáádzoodzíí', Weehee, shicheii, shá dįįh ńléeh, bijiní jiní. Nigo shá dįįh ńléeh, sitsói, hałní jiní. Hajaat'ah-dóó ání jiní, níłch'i biyázhí. Ni dóó ałtsé bá dįįh hińláago nizhónígo néidoołt'oh, hałní jiní. Bíjí áłtsé dįįh yidooléeł nchǫ́'ígií yiih yinł'į[41] yee nínítáá',[41] hałní jiní, níłch'i biyázhí. Nidę́ę'go shá dįįh ńléeh, shicheii, bijiní jiní.

87. T'áá áko nát'ostse' néidii'ą́, jiní. Nát'ohę́ę hayííjaa'ii yiih yiyiijaa', jiní. Bee ndiiltłí'ę́ę néidii'ą́, jiní. Ha'íiłt'i', jiní. Jóhonaa'éí yich'į' dah yidii'ą́, jiní. Tséghádińdíní yę́ę yee yidiiłtła, jiní. Łid ha'íijool, jiní. Yizt'ood, jiní. Yádiłhił yee náánéiyoł, jiní. Náánéizt'ood nahasdzáán yee náánéiyoł, jiní. Náánéizt'ood; yádiłhił yee náánéiyoł. Ni'jí yee yołę́ęjí nanise' yiniiyé át'į́į lá, jiní. Wódahjí yeiyołę́ęjí níłtsą́ biką' yiniiyé át'į́į lá, jiní. Náánéizt'oodę́ę góne' ni'jí nanise' bitádídíín ńdahoodleełii yiniiyé át'į́į lá, jiní. Akéédę́ę' wódahjí yeiyołę́ę dahtoo' náhoodleeł doo índa tó bit'eeshchíí' náhoodleeł doo, éí yiniiyé át'į́į lá, jiní.

88. Dį́į'di yiit'oodgo[41] dį́į'di anłneeh, bijiní jiní. Ákwíí yiilaa, jiní. Dį́į'di yizt'oodgo dį́į'di ayííłna', jiní. Hainí'ą́, jiní. Aadóó bizhniiłt'oh, jiní. Ałtso ńjííłt'oh, jiní. Baa názhní'ą́, jiní. Haah, ní jiní. Ni k'ad shá dįįh nileéh, sitsói, hałní jiní. Dootł'izhii nát'ostse'ę́ę nízhdii'ą́, jiní. Nát'oh hajííjaa', jiní. Biih jííjaa', jiní. Tséghádińdínii yę́ę nízhdii'ą́, jiní. Jóhonaa'éí bich'į' dashdii'ą́, jiní. Nát'ohę́ę bidizńtsih, łid haa ííjool, jiní. Dzizt'ood, jiní. Nahasdzáán bee jiiyoł, jiní. Náádzízt'ood, jiní. Yádiłhił bee jiiyoł, jiní. Náádzízt'ood, jiní. Nahasdzáán bee náájííyoł, jiní. Náádzízt'ood. Yádiłhił bee náájííyoł, jiní.

89. Áłtséédą́ą' nahasdzáán bee jiiyołę́ę nanise' biniiyé ájít'į, jiní. Ákóne' dego bee jiiyołę́ę níłtsą́ biką' biniiyé ájít'į, jiní. Ákóne' nahasdzáán bee náájííyołę́ę nanise' bihádídíín náhoodleeł doo biniiyé ájít'į, jiní. Akéedi dego beezhdeeyołę́ę dahtoo' tó bit'eeshchííh náhoodleeł doo biniiyé ájít'į, jiní.

90. Aajį' ákódzaa, jiní. Kwe'é bee nich'į' haasdzí'ę́ę, ntł'iz éí shiyeel dooleeł biniiyé ádíshní, hałní jiní. Niyeel lá doo ni, shicheii, bijiní jiní.

Lą́'ąą, sitsóí, ní jiní. Doo lá asohodoobéezh da ni, níhwííłbį́įhí wolyéii, hałní jiní. T'óó biza' iildéehii óolyé, ní jiní. Na'azhǫǫsh lá yee' haa honiłné ni, ní jiní. Dá'áka tsosts'idí lá yee haa honiłné ni, ní jiní. Náhást'éí lá jooł yii' néidléehgo[43] yee haa honiłné ni', ní jiní. Jáád yee haa honiłné, sitsóí, hałní jiní. Éí lá azhą́ ákódaat'ée ndi, bijiní jiní. Díí jádígíí biniiyé ádíshní, bijiní jiní. Jó éí áájí aghá yee honiłné. Éí bididíínił, sitsóí, hałní jiní. Índa asdzą́ niyííłbį́įhii[44] éí neezná. T'áá bí éí naaki, áko naakits'áada baa ákéí, hałní jiní, kodóó baa nohkaigo. Íishjááá baa ákéí nizhónígo niidoonił, ní jiní. Ni dó' nahdę́ę́' ndíínił, ní jiní. Kwe'é doo ni ch'ídeesháał da, sitsóí, hałní jiní. Bee shił ééhózin yisht'íinii dó', jiní. Ńláh k'ad, sitsóí, tį', hałní jiní.

[43]This should read: *néiłtéehgo*, because of *nahasht'eii* field rat, which requires the stem *téeh*.

[44]Perfect form. Present tense.

17. Tsé noolch'óshii tsíłkéí

91. Aadóó dashdiikai jiní. Ńt'éé' ákǫ́ǫ́ tsélátahgóó ła' dah njighá, jiní. Hak'i náájíkai, jiní. Tsé noolch'óshii tsíłkéí ájít'įį lá, jiní. Kohaniigi nihokáá' diné doo naagháa da. Ha'át'éédęę́' wohkah, jiní jiní. Níwíiłbįįhí yee' bich'į' deekai, shicheii, jiní jiní. Da' ch'ał hastiin baa nohkai, sitsói, hałní jiní. Daa hoolyé, sitsói, ákwe'é, ní jiní. Hóla, doo shił béého̜zin da, bijiní jiní. Nił ch'íhodeesh'ááł, sitsói, hałní jiní. Lą́'ąą, shicheii shił ch'íhoní'aahínee', bijiní jiní. Da' k'adii yoołgaii hólǫ́, ní jiní. Hólǫ́ǫ́ lá, bijiní jiní. Éí shiyeel dooleeł, ní jiní. Aoo', shił ch'íhoní'aah, bijiní jiní. Dá'ák'eh jiigishí lá hoolyé ni, ní jiní.

92. Dah náázhdiikai, jiní. Aadóó náás t'áá nízaad ninááj ík ai, jiní. Ákohgo t'áá áyídí hadziih, jiní. Ńt'éé' tsédááhgóó ła' nnáájídááh, jiní. Hak'i náájíkai jiní. K'adshą' tsé noolch'óshiiłchíí' tsíłkęęłı ájít'įį lá, jiní. Bich'į' njíkai, jiní. Ńt'éé' ayóigo ch'ídeeldloh. T'áá yidlohdęę́' haadzíí', jiní. Kohaniigi nihokáá' diné doo naagháa da, ní jiní. Níhwíiłbįįhí yee' bich'į' deekai, bijiní jiní. Shí lá shił béého̜zin ni, níhwíiłbįįhí sizįįgi, ní jiní. Doo lá asohodoobéezh da ni, sitsói, hałní jiní. Nił ch'íhodeesh'ááł, sitsói, hałní jiní. Lą́'ąą, shicheii, hágoónee', shił ch'íhoní'aah, bijiní jiní. Da' k'adii diichiłí hólǫ́, sitsói, hałní jiní. Hólǫ́ǫ́ lá, shicheii, bijiní jiní. Lą́'ąą, sitsói, ní jiní. Jó éí shiyeel doo lá, ní jiní.

93. Kodóó bich'į' ninohkaigo sik'is, nididooniił. Ęęgí, ęęgí, nididooniił bijáád níidootįįł, hałní jiní. T'áá áko ńléí asdzánígíí yich'į' ch'ídidooldloh, ní jiní. T'ááká bich'į' ch'ídoołdlóóh lágo, yówehí bee yóweh, hałní jiní. T'óó bik'ee yaa ádoo'níił, hałní jiní. Ákwe'éshą' deit'é, shicheii, bijiní jiní, dinédęę́'. Yich'į' ch'ídeeldlohgo nąąh nahodookał, doo nitah hwiidoonaał da. Éí bąą yówehí bee yóweh, hałní jiní. Jó kwe'é ánáádí'ní jiní. Ni dó' baa ákéígíí bich'į' ch'ídidííldloh, t'áá ałtso nich'į' deidoodloh, hałní jiní. Doo bitah hwiidoonaał da, ní jiní. Bąąh náhodookał, ní jiní. Lą́'ąą ákót'éé lá, shicheii, bijiní jiní. K'ad lá nááneiikah doo ni, shicheii, bijiní jiní. Aadóó nihinááj íkai, jiní.

18. Naashjé'ii hastiin

94. Kǫ́ǫ́ t'áá áyídígo bikin háá'á, jiní, tsé biyaa hanii'áhí hoolyéegi kéé'hat'į́įgo jiní. Naashjé'iidzilí hoolyéegi náázdeeskai, jiní. Ńt'ée'go, shshd, hojiní jiní. Dah náázhdiikai ńt'éé', shshd, náhozhdi'ní jiní. Dah náázhdiikai, ńt'éé', shshd, náhozhdi'ní jiní. Dah náázhdiikai, ńt'éé, shshd, náhozhdi'ní, jiní dį́į'di. Hakééjígo t'áá hayaajį' bił ajííghal. Ńt'éé' áadi ła' hajiyíítį, jiní. Tį', shiba' woh'ash ńlááji'. T'áá ákwe'é shiba' sookée doo, jiní jiní. Áajį' dah nízdiidzá, jiní. Ńt'éé' ńléí wóyahdi dzizdá, jiní. Yah aninááh, sitsói, hałní jiní. Ha'át'íí lá shicheii ahodiyootsází yee'. Ha'át'éegoshą' adeesháál, bijiní jiní. Hótsaago át'é, sitsói, níini yiisoł jiní. Ajííyá, jiní, akóyah. Naashjé'ii hastiin ájít'į́į lá, jiní.

95. Kohaniigi nihookáá' diné doo naagháa da. Ha'át'éédę́ę́'shą' yínáál, sitsói, hałní jiní. Níhwííłbįįhí lá bich'į' déyá ni, shicheii, bijiní jiní. Doo lá asohodoobéezh da ni, sitsói. Baa hidizhnikááh lá, sitsói, ní jiní. Náá'azhǫǫsh lá[45] yee níhwííłbįįh ni, ní jiní. Dá'áka tsosts'idí lá yee níhwííłbįįh ni,[46] ní jiní. Jooł lá yee níhwííłbįįh ni, kóhoníłtsogo bighá hoodzą́ągo, ákóne' jooł yigháikałgo yee níhwííłbįįh, ní jiní. Bijáád lá yee níhwííłbįįh ni bił ałghazhdit'ashgo haadiilwo'go yee níhwííłbįįh, ní jiní. Ńléí dá'ák'eh jigishí hoolyéegiísh yíníyá, hałní jiní. Ákwe'é lá níyáa ni, shicheii, bijiní jiní. Ch'ał hastiin ha'át'íí nilní, hałní jiní. Shí lá yee ntsékeesii áníinii shił béého̱zin, ní jiní. Weeheénee', shicheii, shił ch'íní'aah, bijiní jiní.

96. Da' k'adii bááshzhinii hólǫ́ nit'į, hałní jiní. Hólǫ́ǫ́ lá, shicheii, bijiní jiní. Lą́'ąą, ní jiní. Ńléídę́ę́' diyin dine'é bik'i jiyiiyáhąą t'áá ałtso

[45] *Lą́....ni* is one thing or is another, etc.

[46] *Ni*, I am positive, he is wont to do it, it is a known fact that he does.

áłah dooleeł, hałní[47] jiní. Sis naajiní bilátahdę́ę́' áłah dooleeł. Ayáásh dine'é, dólii dine'é áłah dooleeł, hałní jiní. Tsodził bilátahdę́ę́' táshch'ozh dootł'izh dine'é áłah dooleeł, ní jiní. Dook'o'oosłííd bilátahdę́ę́' ayáásh ch'ozhghálii dine'é áłah dooleeł, ní jiní. Dibé ntsaa bilátahdę́ę́' anilt'ánii dine'é áłah dooleeł, ní jiní. Táłtł'áh náhálgai hoolyéédę́ę́' tó dine'é áłah dooleeł, ní jiní. Dził k'ii'íígai hoolyéédę́ę́' ii'ni' dine'é áłah dooleeł, ní jiní. Tó naagai hoolyéédóó táłtł'áh ha'aléėh dine'é áłah dooleeł, ní jiní. Éí áłah silį́į́'go kodóó áajį' ndoohkah, sitsói, ní jiní. T'áá éí diné yik'eh didoodleeł ńlááh, sitsói, ní jiní.

97. Dah nízdiidzá hach'ą́ą́h na'astł'ǫ́ǫ́ lá, jiní. Béésh diłhiłę́ę hacheii haíńláhą́ą áza'joolkaad beijiiyoł, jiní. Bitł'ólę́ę nááłdááz, jiní. Háádzisdzá. Yaa'adeiz'ą́ągo ajííyáa ni. Áko shį́į t'áá íídą́ą' ayíílo' lá jiní. T'áá ákóyah hwiiską́ągo át'éé lá, jiní. Sitsói, t'áásh ákót'ée dooleeł. Shitł'óól shá hadaałt'é ánánídléėh, hałní jiní. Nínísáa'go ndéí áhoodzaago níká adeeshwoł, hałní jiní. Lą́'ąą, shicheii, bijiní jiní. Bitł'ólę́ę bich'į' dashdiiyá, jiní. Dį́į́'di bik'izhdeejéé', jiní. Bił ahízdeesnii', jiní. Hadaałt'é násdlį́į́', jiní. T'áá aaníí diyin dine'é nílį́į lá, sitsói, tį'ę́ęnee', hałní jiní.

[47] Spider is not directly addressing the hero, but is repeating a current report. The preceding sentence is therefore part of the narrative and *hałní* is rather misleading as compared to the following which indicates Spider's speech.

19. Níhwííłbįįhí

98. Haa lá hoodzaa asdząą́ la' bił yishk'ahnii dziniizį́į'ii dashdiiyá, jiní. T'óó joołkah, jiní, asdzání yę́ę. Ch'ilátah hózhóón yiyiiníishgo ałts'ą́ąjí dińtąądgóó íí'áázh lá, jiní. Ńt'éé' kǫ́ǫ siké, jiní. Bizhníłkááh, jiní. Ostsidii nilínę́ę dah hiitįįhídą́ą' dah yoołjoł, jiní. Akéédę́ę' nilínę́ę tł'éé' iigahí dah yoołjoł, jiní. Yúu, ha'át'éejí lá naninaá ńt'éé', hałní jiní. Dah dzaagóó yee' nihiiską́, níi ni dah hitįhídą́ą' yee náhodííłtsxas, jiní. Akéédę́ę' nilínę́ę hanáánádzíí', jiní. Ha'át'íí lá baa nannáago dáádzaahgóó nihiiską́, níi ni tł'éé' iigahí yee náhodííłtsxas, jiní. Áyídígo kǫ́ǫ hadziih, tį', bizhdííniid jiní. Zǫ zǫ zǫ zǫ, yiists'ą́ą', jiní. Níyol nihí dah diilwod, jiní.

99. Éí yee' ha'ídíl'į́į' lá, jiní, ńlááhdę́ę'. Hajaat'ahdóó níłch'i biyázhí yę́ę ání, jiní. Bich'į' handzih, hałní jiní. T'áadoo ádaat'íní níłch'i dine'é áłtsé ádahodoolzééh, bizhdííniid jiní. Áko shį́į ńléí tooji hwiidzohdi dáádiniláii nilínę́ę hoshdódii bikáa'gi azdeezkaad lá jiní. Hazhool bik'ijį' nazhnííłdee' lá, jiní, níhwííłbįįhí. Bił niizį́į'go bił yah o'ooldee', jiní. Haah, ní jiní. Haa lá hoodzaa, sik'is. T'áadoo hadi'nch'į́į da lá, ní jiní. Hach'į' dah diiyá, jiní. Ęęg, ęęg, níigo bijáád hwiiztą́, jiní. T'áá áko bich'į' dah diiyáii hajáád bidzíztą́, jiní.

100. Weehee', háí shį́į sik'is na'azhǫǫsh daats'í, ní jiní. Éísh yáa be'ádoolnííł. Éí doo sih da, bijiní jiní. Nahgóó ts'aa' yee dá'áka tsosts'idí nínéiníką́, jiní. Éísh yáa be'ádoolnííł, éí doo sih da, náábizhdoo'niid jiní. Be'ekalí yę́ę nahgóó jooł yił ninánéi'nil. Díí daats'í, ní jiní. Éísh yáa be'ádoolnííł, éí doo sih da, náábizhdoo'niid jiní. Lą́'ąą, ní jiní. Weehee', nahá'ákéí ałk'ijį' doo, ní jiní. Náhookǫs bitsijí ba'ákéí ńt'i', jiní. Hó éí shádi'ááh bich'ijí, jiní. Ńléí háí shį́į t'áá nínízinígíí

ńdiiniíł bił ałk'ijį' doo, hałní jiní. Ńléí aníídę́ę́' sikéhígi diné éí ayóó'áyó'ní, jiní jiní. Níłch'i biyázhí hajaat'ahdę́ę́' éí bizhdííniid, jiní.

101. Dooládó' ayói áńt'ée da lá, sik'is, hałní jiní. Weehee', ałghá dadiit'ash ya', sik'is, hałní jiní. Éí diné nas'áhígíí ts'ídá ałtso dabidoonááł. K'ad t'áá łáhídi nich'į' hanáánásdzih, bijiní jiní. Lą́'ąą, hágoshį́į́, shich'į' handzih, sik'is, ní jiní. Éísh asdzánígíí biniinaa hayi' hoołch'iih doo, bijiní jiní. Weehee', sik'is, ha'át'éegi shį́į́ ábidiní, ní jiní. Jó t'áá nihizhihí ałk'ijį' doo, bijiní jiní. Nihijéí ałk'ijį' doo, bijiní jiní. Nihitsiits'iin ałk'ijį' doo, bijiní jiní. Lą́ągo lá hojiníi nin,[48] ní jiní. Tį', jiní, jáák'ehjį'.

[48]Sandoval suggests to change this to read: *áko lá hojiníi łeh,* which is a common expression in narratives. The informant's phrasing is unusual.

20. Jáád

102. Hágoshį́į́ ałts'ą́ą́jí t'óó ahayóigo jil'aah dzizlį́į́', jiní. Ńlááhjí hazhdiijaa', jiní. Bí dó' kojí hadiijaa', jiní. Baa ákéí yę́ę kojį' ńt'i',[49] jiní. Hó éí kojí sikée yee', jiní. Ajííghal, jiní. Náádeelk'id lá, jiní, t'áá áyídígi. Nááyówehdi náádeelk'id lá, jiní. Ákohgo naakigo náádeelk'id. Ńléí t'áá yówehdi náádeelk'id lá, jiní. Ńléí t'áá yówehdi náábi'oh náneełnéehdi náádeelk'id lá. Ákohgo dį́į́' náádeelk'id lá, jiní. Áadi dził si'ą́ooyee',[50] jiní. Dził dah ha'oołii hoolyéé lá, jiní.

103. Áko ch'ał hastiin kǫ́ǫ́ njighá, jiní. Na'ashjée'ii hastiin dó' kǫ́ǫ́ njighá, jiní. Shí hodeessoh, jiní jiní. Sitsóóké, ałgha diit'ash, jiní jiní. Ńléídę́ę́' diné bich'į'go hozdeezoh, jiní, na'ashjéé'ii hastiinę́ę. Nahí diné ahaa naakaigo ch'ał hastiinę́ę hatsóí bijeezhnoolne', jiní. T'ááká ahideelnáolyeed[51] lágo, sitsóí, jiní jiní. Daa lá nít'į́į ndi náhookǫs bich'ijí oo'óolyeed lágo, jiní jiní. Bitsi' noólyeed lágo. Bíni'dii t'áá naaghá hidííłtį́įhgo t'óó bik'ehígo yílwoł doo, jiní jiní. Éí náádeelk'idii-dóó índa doo bíká dííłííł da díí hoodzohjį', k'ad ńlááh, hojiní jiní.

104. Hoodzo yę́ę yikáá' ndeel'eez, jiní. Hó dó' hoodzo yę́ę bikáá' nizdeel'eez, jiní. Aadóó diné hahinoolchą́ą́' ahąąh daneezhteezhí yee', jiní.

105. T'áá dooda dó' hodíína'í ńléí ła' yílk'idę́ę báhátis, jiní. Nááyówehdi náánálk'id bánááhátis, jiní. Nááńléí yówehdi táá'

[49] This would read better: *ńlááhjí ńt'i'*, on the other side in a line (Sandoval).

[50] Sandoval finds no added meaning in the lengthened vowel of *są'áooyee'*, nor in the suffix *yee'*. Perhaps "far off in the distance a mountain stood, he noticed" would be in harmony with the context.

[51] Instead of *ahideelnáolyeed* which gives the sense of running back and forth, Sandoval prefers *ałnáolyeed*, don't cross from your side to his.

yílk'idę́ę báhátis, jiní. Ńléí yówehdi dį́į́' yílk'idę́ę báhátis, jiní, t'áá ahąąh. Ńléí dził si'ánę́ę binaa jiní. T'áadoo dó' hodíína'í ch'íńjį́į́' t'áá ahąąh. Wóshdę́ę́' náádeelk'idę́ę ła' átsé hadziswod, jiní. Akéédę́ę́' ła' hanáádzíswod, jiní. Áko dząądi diné yíl'áhą́ą shį́į́ kodóó deezhchąą'í ńléí ła' yílk'idę́ę yighą́ą'jį' hanásą́ą' léi' áá diné yíl'á, jiní. Háidashą' át'į, dajiní jiní. Níhwííłbįįhí daats'í ałą́ąjį' yilwoł, daaní jiní. Ats'os bee bighaní daats'í ałą́ąjį' yilwoł, doo bééhózin da, dajiní jiní.

106. Naaki yíłk'idę́ę aadę́ę́' jiní. T'áá ahiłtsih diił'áago ahinoołchééł, jiní. Áko shį́į́ ch'ał hastiinę́ę díí hatsóí yilwołjí t'áadoo njizhlizh da. Níhwííłbįįhí yilwołjí t'éí njizhlizh lá, jiní, táá' náádeelk'idę́ę. Ńt'éé' t'áá íiyisí ahoo'nił, t'áá áko ndi níhwííłbįįhí t'áá aghá hidííłtį, jiní. Haa ákééhę́ę ńláahdi hááhgóóshį́į́ áálnii' silį́į́', jiní. Bí éí baa ákééhę́ę bił dahóózhǫǫd, jiní. Kodę́ę'go ńláahdi diné ninánichąą' hoodzoi yę́ę biláahdi, jiní. Náádeelk'idę́ędóó wóshdę́ę́' ahaah dashneezhteezh hoodzoi yę́ę bich'į'. T'áá áko ndi t'áá hagháhidííłtį, jiní. Táa'di ninááididooltał hadziihgo níhwííłbįįhí yę́ę átsidíígo'[52] t'áá áła háaji yee' hanáálwod t'áá áko. Hoodzoi yę́ę[53] kǫ́ǫ́ hoodzohgo t'óó biniit'aajį nizhdeeltáalgo kwe'é nááneezghal, jiní. Báhátis jidooltáál, jiní, łahjígóó. Bijí éí ałníi'gi ndeeltáál lá, jiní, hoodzoi yę́ę.

107. Hach'ooníhę́ę hááhgóó shį́į́ doowosh hayííłne', jiní. Ch'ał hastiinę́ę éí ńjishzhiizh, jiní. Níhwííłbįįhí bi'ashiiké ałtso yaa díneest'ą́, jiní. Nahí naaghá, jiní. Hááhgóó shį́į́ naa ńdooyiihgo kojí dó' ákót'é, jiní. T'áá áko bitsénił ha'át'íí shį́į́ óolyé, tsénił ndizéehii[54] néidii'ą́, jiní, baa hizhdiilyeed ndi éí bee ádił ninádeijiilne' lá, jiní. Weehee', hágoshį́į́ t'ah sídohdą́ą́', ní jiní. Bił nízhdiilwod, jiní. Hach'į' dah díníit'ą́, jiní. Hágoshį́į́, hałní jiní. Bee bits'iiyah iijííłne', jiní. T'áadoo ééhózini bitsiits'iin jíítseed, jiní. Áko shį́į́ dah yiitįįhí yootsoh bizéédéé'ą́ągo diits'a'go ninálwo'ę́ę t'áá íídą́ą́' bił hajoolwod lá, jiní.

[52] *Átsidíígo'*, not a real collapse but some interference, as though his foot gave out, checking his speed.

[53] This seems superfluous, unless *kóhoodzohgo* be omitted. I have tried to retain it in the free translation. The sense is not destroyed by rendering: When he stepped just next to the line which had been drawn he was again checked. On his side (of the track), etc.

[54] *Ńdiizéehii*, movable but not removable, such as a tree stump. The informant explains that in striking, the axe would bound back upon the person wielding it. The Gambler therefore usually allowed the winners to kill themselves in this manner.

108. Diné bikáa'gi dįį'di bił ałk'i jilwod aadóó ńléí waa' dashdiijaa'ą́ągóó bił ajoolwod, jiní. Bitsiits'iinęę biyi'dę́ę́' k'aalógii ha'ísol, jiní. Bee nahoolzhiizhdi k'aalógiiłgaii háàyá, jiní. Ch'ilátah hózhóón bitahgóó kódaadzaa, jiní, k'aalógii yę́ę. Bikéédóó k'aalógiiłgaii yę́ę t'óó doo hatah hwiinááńígóó ajííyá, jiní. Hajaat'ahdóó níłch'i biyázhí yę́ę áhální, jiní. Ńléí hajáád haisíníłbánę́ę éí ájít'į níhwííłbįįhí yę́ę k'aalógiiłgaii bee dashdiiyá, ní jiní. Aajį' baa ákéé yę́ę doo baa ńdzíst'įįd da, jiní. Hó éí haa ákééhę́ę dah nízhdii'eezh, jiní. Aajį' ałtso táá'oosdee'.

21. Ii'ni' dine'é

109. Aadóó dah náázhdiikai, jiní. Dził łigai hoolyéí bikáá' hasdee'; ii'ni' dine'é kééhat'įį lá, jiní. Atsiniltł'ish yit'įį lá, jiní. Kohaniigi nihookáá' diné doo naagháa da. Ha'át'éédę́ę́' lá wohkah, hałní jiní. Jó łahgo shił ch'íhodíí'áałgo éí biniiyé ásht'į, shicheii, bijiní jiní. Lą́'ąą, sitsóí, ní jiní. Łahgo lá nił ch'íhodeesh'ááł ni, sitsóí, ní jiní. Woohóń[55] ádííńjí, hałní jiní. Ats'os yee bighan lá, dashiłníi ni, shicheii, bijiní jiní. Díí shiinéé'ígíí bik'ehgo ádaał'įį dooleeł, bee náás wohkah doo, hałní jiní. Yoołkááłgóó díí bee náás wohkah doo, hałní jiní. Díí tsinígíí[56] yiisíįhii[57] éí ádaał'įį doo, hałní jiní. Da' bááshzhinii hólǫ́, hałní jiní. Hólǫ́ǫ́ lá, bijiní jiní. Da' dootł'izhii hólǫ́ nit'į, hałní jiní. Hólǫ́ǫ́ lá, bijiní jiní. Da' diichiłí nit'į, hałní jiní. Hólǫ́ǫ́ lá, bijiní jiní. Da' yoołgaii nit'į, hałní jiní. Hólǫ́ǫ́ lá, bijiní jiní. Yoołkááłgóó nihookáá' diné wolyéí bich'ą́ąh áníléehgo bááshzhinígíí naaki dooleeł, ní jiní. Diné bik'i nahagháago ntł'iz ashdla' shiyeel doo, ní jiní. Asdzání bik'i nahagháago díí ntł'izígíí t'áá bíighahgo yoołgaiígíí naakigo, éí bił ashdla'go shiyeel doo, ní jiní. Índa t'áá shindii'a'[58] t'áá éí t'áá dįį'dę́ę́' dahoohtiih doo, ní jiní. Índa binaa t'áá shá bik'ehgo ch'il dah hidoołchíih doo. Dįį'di nahidilchíihgo bíighah ni'iileeh doo, ní jiní.

[55] Instead of *weeheé nee'*.

[56] The suffix *ígíí* particularizes *tsin*, "that particular tree" or the "specific tree." In the English translation this specification may often be ignored.

[57] *Yiisíįhii*, which I have sanctified, or set aside as sacred. Since this has reference to striking by lightning, we have rendered: which I have struck.

[58] *Shindii'a'*, my upright, that is, the tree which I have struck.

110. Kojí náhookǫs bich'ijí éí doo ahijígháah da, ní jiní. Nchǫ́'ígíí hainít'íinii ákǫ́ǫ́ ch'íhéjeeh, ní jiní. Índa t'áá éí ha'a'aahjį' deez'áí, éí honeeshgish doo, ní jiní. T'áá éí shádi'ááhjį' deez'áí, éí dó' honeeshgish doo, ní jiní. T'áá éí e'e'aahjį' deez'áí, t'áá éí honeeshgish doo, ní jiní. T'áá éí náhookǫsjį' deez'áí t'áá éí honeeshgish doo, ní jiní. Índa t'áá éí azhííh bąąh hadǫ́ǫzii t'áá éí dó', ní jiní. Índa t'áá éí tsin dii'a'ígíí ła' dishłidii t'áá éí dó' choidaoł'įį doo, ní jiní. Índa tsin nináhoneel'ą́ąjį' ts'ídá t'áá ałtso danihitł'éel doo, ní jiní. Kwe'é índa bich'į' hadzoodzíí', jiní. Ha'át'íí dadii'níigo danihitł'éel doo, bijiní jiní. Kwe'é sin ła' há hadoot'ą́, jiní.

111. K'ad yich'į' neezdá, ii'ni' diłhił k'ad yich'į' neezdá,
Atsiniltł'ish bits'ą́ą' náhádiłgo ninháhádił dóó tsin ninádadeesgaigo áyoolííł.
K'ad bicháníiłheelígo k'ad bits'á jílgishígo, tó bits'á neeltiinígo áyoolííłgo, k'ad yich'į' neezdá.

112. Ii'ni' dootł'izh k'ad yich'į' neezdá.
Hatsoo yilghał bits'ánáhádił dóó tó ńdadeesgaigo áyoolííł.
K'ad bichádaasxeelígo hatsoo yilghaal bits'ánahadiłígo tó bits'á-neeltiingo k'ad yich'į' neezdá yéé-éé-ya-hee-yí, ánii yóo.[59]

113. Díí k'adígíí nihaa deet'ą́ągo bee oolk'ą́. Áko ha'át'éego níídéeshiiłgo niyeel ádeeshłííł, bijiní jiní. K'os látah sidiilts'įhí ii'ni' diłhił tsíłkę́ę́h naat'áanii niyeel áshłaa, shidid íiniił, hałní jiní. K'os látah sidiilts'įhí ii'ni' dootł'izh ch'ikę́ę́h naat'áanii niyeel áshłaa, shididíiniił, ní jiní. K'os látah sidiilts'įhí ii'ni' łitso tsíłkę́ę́h naat'áanii niyeel áshłaa, shididíiniił, ní jiní. K'os látah sidiilts'įhí ii'ni' łigai ch'ikę́ę́h naat'áanii niyeel áshłaa, shididíiniił, ní jiní. Aajį' ałtso hoł ch'ét'ą́.

[59]From the invocations mentioned in the following, it appears that two stanzas have been omitted: *ii'ni' łitso*, Yellow, and *ii'ni' łigai*, White Thunder.

22. Ayáásh bąąh nanoogáád

114. Aadóó dah náázhdiikai, jiní. Sisnaajiní bilátahjį' hanáádzískai, jiní. Ayáásh dine'é kééhat'įį lá, jiní. Koo haniigi nihookáá' diné doo naagháa da, ní jiní. Łahgo shił ch'íhodíí'áałgo lá éí biniiyé asht'į ni, shicheii, bijiní jiní. Da' k'adii doo k'aak'ehii hóló, ní jiní. Hóló, bijiní jiní. Da' k'adii bitsii'jį' t'áá bééhózin, hałní jiní. T'áá lá bééhózin ni, bijiní jiní. Bitsii'jį' bitáa'gi da' dootł'izh béstł'ó, ní jiní. Hólóó lá, áko lá át'é ni, bijiní jiní. Éí lá shiyeeł dooleeł ni. Éí bideená nił ch'íhodeesh'ááł, hałní jiní.

115. Ha'át'éegi shįį bee nił ééhózingo ninááʼ, shicheii, bijiní jiní. Nizhónígo lá ntséskeesgo naasháa ni, sitsóí, ní jiní. Jó díí shaa ndanohháadgo tádídíín shaa ndanohháadgo díí jish dabidohnínígíí bee hadadít'éego ndaohłéeh doo, hałní jiní. Índa dootł'izhígíí tádídíín bił sizah ndaah'áago[60] éí nihizéé' si'ąągo bee sodadoołzin doo, hałní jiní. Índa shijét'iizhígíí ádaohłe'go éí bee íists'ąą' baa naahkai doo, ní jiní. Éí lá ábidishní ni, shicheii, bijiní jiní. Sisnaajiní t'áá éí yoołkáálgóó chóídaoł'įį doo, ní jiní. Akwe'é bééhosihya' lá, hái shįį éí jinínęę.

116. Aadóó t'áá áko dah náázhdiikai tsoodził bich'į'. Tsoodził bilátahgi hanáádzískai. Diné t'óó dootł'izhígo yęę nináádaakai, jiní. Táshchizh dootł'izh dine'é ádaat'įį lá, jiní. Ha'át'éédęę' lá wohkah. Kohaniigi nihookáá' diné doo naagháa da, hałní jiní. Łahgo shił ch'íhodíí'áałgo lá biniiyé ni, shicheii, bijiní jiní. Da' k'adii dootł'izhii nee hóló, hałní jiní. Hólóó lá, shicheii, bijiní jiní. Éí lá shí shiyeel doo ni, ní jiní. Éí bideená nił ch'íhodeesh'ááł ni, hałní jiní. Da' dził łigaigi shįį nohkai, hałní jiní. Áadi lá niikai ni, bijiní jiní. Da' ii'ni' dine'é baa nohkai, hałní jiní. Ts'ídá bóhólníihęę doo nihił ch'íní'ąą da, sitsóí, hałní jiní. Lą'ąą, shicheii, hágoónee'. Shił ch'íní'aah, bijiní jiní.

117. T'áá bindii'a' yiisįįhii ndii'ááh ádaoł'įį doo, hałní jiní. Doo lá shił ch'íní'ąą da, shicheii, bijiní jiní. Díí lá tsoodził wolyé ni, sitsóí, hałní jiní. Kwe'é lá yá yáhóóką hoolyé ni, ní jiní. Lą'ąą, shicheii, bijiní jiní. Náás yoołkáałgóó kodóó t'éí jish ál'įį doo, hałní jiní. Kodóó t'éí k'eet'áán yáłti' ál'įį doo, ní jiní. Lą'ąą, shicheii, éí lá biniiyé ásht'į ni, bijiní jiní.

[60]It is then called: *dólii bizaa nastáán*, put into Bluebird's mouth. This is a turquoise which has been placed into a Bluebird's mouth, then rolled in pollen.

23. Tééhoołtsódii bighangi

118. Aadóó nihinááji̇́kai, jiní, ndi t'áadoo ha'át'ii da bik'i náá'iildéhí tá łtł'ááh náhálgai hoolyéegi nááji̇́kai, jiní. Ch'é'étiinjį' ńjíkai, jiní. Shá bitł'ájiłchíí hoolyéí dáádińláá lá, jiní. Ákóne' yah ajookai, jiní. Ńt'éé' wóniigóó téé hoołtsódii sitįį́ lá, jiní. Ha'át'éédéę́' lá wohkah. Kohanii nihookáá' diné doo naagháa da, ní jiní. Jó łahgo shił ch'íhodíí'áałgo éí biniiyé ásht'į, shicheii, bijiní jiní. Lą'ąą, ní jiní. Ha'a'aahjį'go tádiłhił ahííyį, jiní. Nááts'íílid agodí yę́ę néidiilá, jiní. Tádiłhił ahííyínę́ę yee nayiisnáá'dóó de áyiilaa. Ńt'éé' dáádiníbaal át'éé lá, jiní.

119. Bik'izhnaghal, jiní. Téé łįį́' eel'á, jiní. Ha'át'ii át'é nínízin, sitsói, hałní jiní, hajaat'ahdóó nílch'i biyázhí yę́ę éí yee níká diisxilii át'é téé łįį́' bidiní, hałní jiní. Doo béédíńtą́ą́'góó t'áá aajį' dííleeł. Éí yąą ání, hałní jiní. Jó téé łįį́' át'é, shicheii, bijiní jiní. Éí lá át'é ni, sitsói, hałní jiní. Naghái éí ha'át'ii át'é, hałní jiní, ha'a'aahjí ahideełná[61] dah siláago. Hajaat'ahdóó ánáádí'ní, jiní, nílch'i biyázhí, Jó atsinitł'ish ahideełná dah silá bidiní, hałní jiní. Jó atsiniltł'ish ahideełná dah silá, shicheii, jiní jiní. Éí lá át'é ni, sitsói, hałní jiní.

120. Shádi'áahjį'go dah náádiidzá tádootł'izh anááhííyį, jiní. T'áá yee kóyiilaa yę́ę yee kónááyiidlaa, jiní. Yee de ánááyiidlaa, jiní. Ákóne' anááji̇́ghal, jiní. Ńt'éé' téé łįį́' dootł'izhgo eel'áá' lá, jiní. Ha'át'ii át'é nínízin, sitsói, hałní jiní, hajaat'ahdóó yę́ę. T'áá éí bik'ehgo hanáánádzíí', jiní. Jó téé łįį́' át'é, shicheii, bijiní jiní. Éí lá át'é ni, sitsói, ní jiní. Bikáági ahideełná dah siláhígíí éí ha'át'ii át'é, hałní jiní. Hajaat'ahdóó yę́ę ánáádí'ní jiní. Jó hatsoo alghaał ahideełná dah silá, bidiní, hałní jiní. Jó hatsoo alghaał ahideełná, shicheii, bijiní jiní. Éí lá át'é ni, sitsói, hałní jiní.

[61] *Ahideełná*, side by side with heads reversed.

121. Aadóó e'e'aahjį' dah náádiidzá, jiní. Tá-łitso ahííyįį́ lá, jiní. Yee néidiilnáhą́ą yee néideesnáá', jiní. Yee[62] deg ánáayiidlaa, jiní. Tééłįį́' łitsogo anáánál'a' lá, jiní. Ha'át'íí át'é nínízin, sitsóí, hałní jiní. Hajaat'ahdóó yę́ę anáádí'ní, jiní, níłch'i biyázhí. Jó tééłįį́' át'é, bidiní, hałní jiní. Jó tééłįį́' át'é, shicheii, bizhdííniid jiní. Éí lá át'é ni, sitsóí, hałní jiní. Bikáagi ahideełná dah silái, ha'át'íí át'é nínízin, hałní jiní. Hajaat'ahdóó yę́ę ánáádí'ní jiní. Jó shá bitł'óól ahideełná dah silá, bidiní hałní jiní. Jó shá bitł'óól ahideełná dah silá, shicheii, bijiní jiní. Éí lá át'é ni, sitsóí, ní jiní.

122. T'áá áko náhookǫsjį' dah náádiidzá, jiní. Ńt'éé' táłigai ahííyį, jiní. Yee néidiilnáhą́ą yee néidiisnáá', jiní. Yee deg ánááyiidlaa, jiní. Áajį' ninááddzídzá, jiní. Tééłįį́' łigaigo eel'a' lá jiní. Ha'át'íí át'é nínízin, sitsóí, hałní jiní. Jó tééłįį́', bidiní, hałní jiní, níłch'i biyázhí. Jó tééłįį́' át'é, shicheii, bijiní jiní. Éí lá át'é ni, sitsóí, ní jiní. Bikáagi ahideełná siláhígíí, éí ha'át'íí át'é nínízin, hałní jiní. Jó náátsʼíílid át'é, bidiní, hałní jiní, níłch'i biyázhí. Jó náátsʼíílid at'é, shicheii, bijiní jiní. Éí lá át'é ni, sitsóí, hałní jiní.

123. Áłtséédą́ą́' ha'a'aahjígo de áyiilaaą́ą tééłįį́' diłhiłgo dah nda'ałkǫ́ǫ́', jiní. Shádi'ááhjí de áyiilaaą́ą tádootł'izh biyi'góó tééłįį́' dootł'izhgo dah nda'alkǫ́ǫ́', jiní. E'e'aah biyaají táłitso ayííyínę́ę biyi'góó tééłįį́' łitsogo dah nda'ałkǫ́ǫ́', jiní. Náhookǫs biyaají táłigai ahííyínę́ę biyi'góó tééłįį́' łigaigo dah nda'ałkǫ́ǫ́', jiní. Díí ha'a'aahjí bidáádińláígíí, ha'át'íí át'é nínízin, sitsóí, hałní jiní. Hajaat'ahdóó ájíní jiní, níłch'i biyázhí. Jó tó asaa' diłhił át'é, bidiní, hojiní jiní. Tó áłah náshchíín biyi' hólǫ́ǫgo át'é, bidiní, bijiní jiní. Jó tó asaa' diłhił át'é, tó áłah náshchíín biyi' hólǫ́ǫgo bidáádińlá, bijiní jiní. Éí lá át'é ni, sitsóí, ní jiní.

124. Shádi'ááhjí yę́ę ha'át'íí bidáádińlá nínízin, sitsóí, hałní jiní. Hajaat'ahdóó yę́ę áhojiní jiní. Jó tó asaa' dootł'izh tó biyáázh bii' hólǫ́ǫgo bidáádińlá, jiní jiní. Éí lá át'é ni, sitsóí, ní jiní. E'e'aah biyaají yę́ę, díí ha'át'íí át'é nínízin, hałní jiní. Jó tó asaa' łitso níłtsą́ biką' biyi' hólǫ́ǫgo bidáádińlá, bidiní, hojiní jiní. Jó tó asaa' łitso níłtsą́ biką' bii' hólǫ́ǫgo bidáádińlá, shicheii, bijiní jiní. Éí lá át'é ni, sitsóí, jiní jiní.

[62] Instrumental *yee* seems to imply that he raised the yellow water with the stubby rainbow and that lightnings hovered over the Water Horses at the lake bottom. This is brought out in the two former visits to the dark and blue waters, with a slight change of phrase: "After he had moved the (dark) water he raised it with this (rainbow), as this (water) happened to be a curtain (for Water Horses)."

Náhookǫsjí yę́ę, ha'át'íí bidáádińlá nínízin, hałní jiní. Jó tó asaa' ligai níłtsą́ bi'áád bii' hólǫ́ǫgo bidáádińlá, bijiní jiní. Éí lá át'é ni, sitsóí, hałní jiní. T'áá aaníí diyin dine'é nílį́į lá, sitsóí, hałní jiní.

125. Áko lá t'áá ła' néinisdzinii shił ch'íhoyí'aah, bijiní jiní. Ńléí łahgo doo shíínáał da, shicheii, bijiní jiní. Ha'át'éegi ábidiní, sitsóí, ní jiní. Ła'a tł'éé' hwíintaalgo lá níyáa ni, shicheii, bijiní jiní. T'áá lá aaníí áhódzaa ni, sitsóí, hałní jiní. Áko lá aadę́ę' bee hwíínísáhą́ą t'áá ałtso shił bééhodoozį́įł ni, shicheii, bijiní jiní. Lą́'ąą, sitsóí, ní jiní. Da' k'adii bááshzhinii nit'į, hałní jiní. Hólǫ́ǫ lá, jiní jiní. Da' k'adii dootł'izhii nit'į, ní jiní. Hólǫ́ǫ lá, jiní jiní. Da' k'adii diichiłii nit'į, hałní jiní. Hólǫ́ǫ lá, bijiní jiní. Da' k'adii yoołgaii nit'į, hałní jiní. Hólǫ́ǫ lá, bijiní jiní. Da' k'adii tádzís'eełí nit'į,[63] hałní jiní. Hólǫ́ǫ lá, bijiní jiní. Éí lá shí shiyeel doo ni, ní jiní. Lą́'ąą, shicheii. Éí lá biniiyé ádíshní ni, bijiní jiní.

[63]*Tádzís'eełí* is a white, rather flat conch with red spots (Sandoval). Perhaps a species of abalone.

24. Tóee k'eet'ánígíí

126. Bee shá dįįh nályée dooleełii lá hólǫǫ ni, hałní jiní. K'adshą' k'eet'áán ááh yiłníí lá jiní. Bik'eet'ą' diłhił lá jiní, tééhołtsódii. Naaki bee yéejį'. Dził nát'oh tó nát'oh díí shá biih ńdaohjih doo, ní jiní. Tséghádińdínii shá bee ńdadoołtłi' doo, ní jiní. Tółchiin bídaohtłohgo, ní jiní. Áko baa shił hózhǫǫ doo, ní jiní. Ákóne'é k'eet'áán dootł'izhgo shá ádadoohłííł, ní jiní. Dził nát'oh tó nát'oh shá biih ńdaohjih doo, ní jiní. Tséghádińdínii shá bee ńdadoołtłi' doo, ní jiní, tółchiin bídaohtłohgo, ní jiní. Áko baa shił hózhǫǫ doo, ní jiní.

127. K'ad díí k'eet'ánígíí biih naazhjaa'ii ts'ídá t'áá ałtso ákót'é. Bidadadeest'áanii teeł bihádídíín bee dadadeest'ą́.[64]

128. Téé́łįį' bik'eet'ą' diłhił, jiní, ha'a'aahjí yę́ę, shádi'ááhjí yę́ę, téé́łįį' dootł'izhę́ę bik'eet'ą' dootł'izh jiní. E'e'aahjí yę́ę, téé́łįį' łitsoi yę́ę bik'eet'ą' łitso, jiní. Náhookǫsjí téé́łįį' łigai yę́ę bik'eet'ą' łigai, jiní. Aajį' shijaa' éidí.

129. Ákóne' níłtsą́ ashkii bik'eet'ą' diłhił, jiní. Níłtsá at'ééd bik'eet'ą' dootł'izh, jiní. Hajilgish bik'eet'ą' dootł'izh, jiní. Nááts'íílid yaago bik'eet'ą' dootł'izh, dego łichíí', jiní. Aajį' náánáshjaa'.

130. Ii'ni' diłhił bik'eet'ą' diłhił, jiní. Ii'ni' dootł'izh bik'eet'ą' dootł'izh, jiní. Ii'ni łitso bik'eet'ą' łitso, jiní. Ii'ni' łigai bik'eet'ą' łigai, jiní. Aajį' náánáshjaa'. K'os diłhił bik'eet'ą' diłhił, jiní. K'os dootł'izh bik'eet'ą' dootł'izh, jiní. Tó áłah náshchíín bik'eet'ą' diłhił, jiní. Tó biyáázh bik'eet'ą' dootł'izh, jiní. Aajį' náánáshjaa'.

[64] *K'eet'áán*. The meaning of *k'ee* is uncertain, and *t'áán* perhaps a "joint."

131. Tł'iish áníníğíí bikąʼii bik'eet'ą' diłhił. Tł'iish áníníğíí bi'áadii bik'eet'ą' łigai. Tł'iishk'aa' bikąʼii bik'eet'ą' diłhił. Tł'iishk'aa' bi'áadii bik'eet'ą' dootł'izh.

132. Naal'eełí ntsaaíğíí bikąʼii bik'eet'ą' diłhił. Naal'eełí ntsaaíğíí bi'áadii bik'eet'ą' dootł'izh. Naal'eełí doo naat'a'íğíí bikąʼii bik'eet'ą' diłhił. Naal'éełí doo naat'a'íğíí bi'áadii bik'eet'ą' dootł'izh. Aajįʼ náánáshjaa'.

133. Tábąąsdísítsoh bikąʼii bik'eet'ą' łigai. Tábąąsdísítsoh bi'áadii bik'eet'ą' łibá. Ałtadashjaa'go łibá yileeh. Tábąąsdísí ałts'íísíğíí bikąʼii bik'eet'ą' łigai. Tábąąsdísí áłts'íísíğíí bi'áadii bik'eet'ą' náánalbá. Aajįʼ náánáshjaa'.

134. Daak'įį' bikąʼii bik'eet'ą' łitso; bi'áadii bik'eet'ą' náánálbá. Yá'azhjool bikąʼii bik'eet'ą' dootł'izh; bi'áadii bik'eet'ą' náádootł'izh. Ał'ąą bee wójíidi t'éí t'áá ał'ąą át'é.

135. Tooji noołna bikąʼii bik'eet'ą' łigai; bi'áadii bik'eet'ą' łigai. Bee wójí t'éí t'áá ał'ąą ánáánát'é. Tooji ndiigai bikąʼii bik'eet'ą' łigai; bi'áadii bik'eet'ą' łigai. Bee wójíidi t'éí t'áá ał'ąą.

136. Tooji nahabił bik'eet'ą' łigai bi'áadii bik'eet'ą' łigai. Bee wójí t'éí t'áá ał'ąą, Hoz bikąʼii bik'eet'ą' dootł'izh; bi'áadii bik'eet'ą' łitso.

137. Ch'ał ntsaaíğíí bikąʼii bikeet'ą' diłhił; bi'áadii bik'eet'ą' dootł'izh. Ch'ał nineezí bikąʼii bik'eet'ą' dootł'izh; bi'áadii bik'eet'ą' dootł'izh. Wójíidi t'éí t'áá ał'ąą.

138. Wónaalts'ilí bik'eet'ą' diłhił; bi'áadii bik'eet'ą' dootł'izh. Ts'ǫǫ sánii bik'eet'ą' diłhił; bi'áadii bik'eet'ą' dootł'izh.

139. Tábąąstíín bik'eet'ą' ayaagi łitso, bikáa'gi hadadeesxéél. Bi'áadii t'áá ákónáánát'é; ayaagi náánáltso, bikáa'gi hanáádadeesxéél. Chaa' bik'eet'ą' ałtaahíjaahgo t'óó dinilbáago bikáa'gi hadaastso. Bi'áadii ákónáánát'é.

140. Tsisteeł bik'eet'ą' dootł'izh; bi'áadii bik'eet'ą' dootł'izh ałdóʼ. T'óó t'áá ał'ąą bee wójí. Ch'ééh digháahii bikąʼii bik'eet'ą' diłhił; bi'áadii bik'eet'ą' náádiłhił. T'óó t'áá ał'ąą baa náwójí.

141. Ts'ilghááh bikąʼii bik'eet'ą' łigai, łizhin bee astł'in; bi'áadii bik'eet'ą' łibá, łigai bee astł'in. Tótł'iish bik'eet'ą' diłhił; bi'áadii bik'eet'ą' dootł'izh. Aajįʼ.

142. Aadóó na'ashǫ́ʼii dich'ízhii bik'eet'ą' diłhił; bikąʼii bikáa'gi łigai bee béésh bik'i sinil, ałnáahgo sinil. Bi'áadii bik'eet'ą' łigai bikáa'gi diłhił bee béésh ahideełná sinil.

143. Naashjé'ii bik'eet'ą' diłhił; bi'áadii bik'eet'ą' łibá. Tsé naalch'óshii bik'eet'ą' łibá; bi'áadii bik'eet'ą' łibá. T'áá ał'ąą bee

náánáwójí. Tsé naalch'óshiiłchíí' bik'eet'ą' dootł'izh, bikáa'gi hadaashchii'. Bi'áadii bik'eet'ą' náádootł'izh, bikáa'gi hanáádaashchii'. Wójíhígíí t'áá ał'ąą.

144. K'aalógiiłgai biką'ii bik'eet'ą' łigai, diłhił bee astł'in, dootł'izh bee astł'in, łitso bee astł'in, łichíí' bee astł'in. Bi'áadii bik'eet'ą' łigai. T'áá ałtso bee náánástł'in. Wójíígi t'éí t'áá ał'ąą.

145. Éí aadę́ę́' kót'éego hool'áa ndi ts'ídá ałtso k'eet'áán yáłti' bikéé' íí'á. Ts'ídá ałtso disǫs. Aajį' hoł yiyííłta', jiní. Éí lą́, shicheii, bizhdííniid jiní. Yoołkááłgóó bee náás hoot'ih doo, bijiní jiní. K'adii lá, shicheii, aajį'. Jó shí dishní eii. Azhą́ kót'ée ndi t'áá át'é ádin. Doo ałtso shił yéelta' da.

25. Tóee bee ła' yit'įįgi

146. Jó ńléí tó hodiłt'eehgo jó kwe'é hohodiiłt'ih, jiní. Índa ii'ni'ígíí hohodiiłt'ihgo, índa naadą́'ígíí bits'ą́ądóó téézhdiil'įįhgo, índa teełígíí jííyą́ą'dóó yee hohodiiłt'ih. Teeł bihádídínígíí bił dzideesdzíihgo hazhíí ásdįįdgo hohodiiłt'ih. Éí aajį' ákót'é. Tsin ii'ni' yiidiiłtaa'ii bee ajííyą́ą'go yee hohodidoołt'ih. Índa dibéhígíí ákwííyiilaago jííyą́ą'go yee hohodidoołt'ih. Índa łį́'ígíí ákwííyiilaago jííyą́ą'go yee hohodidoołt'ih. Índa béégashiiígíí ákwííyiilaago jííyą́ą'go yee hohodidoołt'ih. Índa naadą́'ígíí[65] bó'oosni'go jííyą́ą'go yee hohodidoołt'ih. Índa níyoltsoh ńdadikaahgóó tsin hadayiiłtł'iidii bee ájííyą́ą'go hohodidiłt'ih.

147. Jó áko díí éí ákót'éegogo bee ła' yit'į́, jiní. Éí t'áásh át'é adoojah. Jó t'ááłáhí da át'įį łeh. Kojí hwiiłhéehgo habiłígíí éí yee hoł halnih. Tééhołtsódiidę́ę' át'įįgo táłtł'ááh yígo' hojil'į́. Tééhłį́į'dę́ę' át'įįgo táłtł'ááh yígo' hojil'į́. Éí bąą biyeel álnéehgo tééhoołtsódii bik'eet'ą' k'égish. Tééhłį́į'jí dó' ákót'é. Níłtsą́ ashkiijí dó' t'áá ákót'é. Éí bik'eet'ą' higéésh. K'eet'áán k'égish. Ńláahii ntł'iz bits'á'nil, táá' njaa'go. Éí t'áadoo béého̧zini, t'óó táa'go ahidahidinídéeh.

[65] *Yi* low-toned refers to the place or cornpatch, instead of high-toned *gíí* which particularizes.

26. K'eet'áán hadil'įįhgi

148. T'áá áko t'eeshchíí' t'áá háida hólǫǫgo ninááj́íjih. Tádídíín dootł'izh ákóne' ninááj́íjih. Teeł bihádídíín ninááj́íjih. Índa ayáásh t'áá háida t'áá hólónígíí dólii, tsídiiłtsooí da táa'go ninááj́í'nił, bits'a'astsiin ałts'ą́ą́hjí haa'nizh, bitsee' dǫ́'. T'ááłá'ígo haa'nizh. Éí t'áá oot'aahgo wolyé. Ákóne' ats'os łigai ninááj́ídlé. Ákóne' tązhiits'os ninááj́ídlé. Ákóne' tązhii bibe'ezhóó' ninááj́ídlé. Ákóne' tł'óózóół ninááj́ídlé. T'áá áko ąąh nanoogáád, dólii bąąh nanoogáád, aniłt'ánii bąąh nanoogáád. Éí índa k'eet'ánę́ę naakidi bídahizhdeełná. Dólii t'áá hináanii bitsee' haa'nizhii, éí bídahizhdeełná, ats'osę́ę. Éí t'áá ałtso bikáá' naakidi jidiléeh. Aajį' ałtso hadil'įįh.

149. Índa tádídíín nízdiiłtsos. T'ááłá'í nítánígo bikáá' hizhdinił, kodę́ę́' hózhǫǫgo náádidíídlááł, jiníigo. T'áá áyídíjį' náádidíídlááł, jiníigo. T'áá áko diné bik'i nahojiłáii bikétł'ááhdę́ę́' bitsiit'aajį' bąąh ájiił'įįh. Ła' bizaah jijih. Ła' bázhdinił. Díí yikáá'góó naagháa doogo éí ál'į. T'áá áko k'eet'áán bílák'ee jikááh,[66] átséhę́ę ayaadi njikááh. Aadóó ałk'i joo'niłgo akéedi yę́ę akáa'di yileeh. T'áá áko áajį' bich'į' jinidaah. T'áá áko hadzidzih.

150. Táłtł'ááh náhágaigi tééhołtsódii tsíłkę́ę́h[67] naat'áanii niyeel áshłaa, ná dįįh yílá.

T'áá díí jį bee ahół'íinii ni'alíil hąąh háádííléeł, ni'alíil hąąh háinílá.

[66]Denoting a calico spread which is folded and sticks placed upon it. Then it is handed to the patient. Therefore the stem *k'aa'* is used to denote a vessel or tray.

[67]For female prayerstick substitute: *ch'ikę́ę́h naat'áanii* even with female patient. *Dághanáshjin* always mentions male first.

Nízaadgóó hats'á ndííléél, nízaadgóó hats'á néinílá, nízaadgóó bił ńdíídleeł, nízaadgóó bił nisínídlįį'.
Hózhǫǫgo t'áá díí jį náázhdidoodááł, hózhǫǫgo t'áá díí jį hoł hodínook'eeł.
Hózhǫǫgo haa hodidooldooh, hózhǫǫgo njigháa doo.
Hatah honeesk'ázígo njigháa doo, hatah áhoszólígo njigháa doo.
Chánah jílįįgo njigháa doo, doo hąąh tééhgóó njigháa doo, doo hohodééłníígóó njigháa doo.
Hatsiji' hózhǫǫgo njigháa doo,[68] *hakéédęę' hózhǫǫgo njigháa doo.*
Hayaagi hózhǫǫgo njigháa doo, hak'igi hózhǫǫgo njigháa doo, hanaa t'áá ałtso hózhǫǫgo njigháa doo, hazaad hahóózhǫǫdgo njigháa doo.
Są'ah naagháí bik'eh hózhóón jílįįgo njigháa doo.
Hózhǫ́ náhásdlįį', dįį'di (four times).

Tátł'ááh[69] *náhálgaigi tádiłhił bee dah honíkąągi tééłįį' tsíłkéí naat'áanii.... Tádootł'izh*[70] *bee dah honíkąągi tééłįį' ch'ikęęh naat'áanii.... Tátł'ááh.... Tátsoi.... Tééłįį' tsíłkéí naat'áanii.... Táligaii tééłįį' ch'ikęęh naat'áanii....*

Yá'ąąshdi k'os bee hooghandi níłtsą́ ashkii tsíłkęęh naat'áanii.... yá'ąąshdi tó bee hooghandi níłtsá at'ééd ch'ikęęh naat'aanii....

Yá'ąąshdi hajilgish tsíłkęęh naat'áanii.... Yá'ąąshdi hajilgish ch'ikęęh naat'áanii.... Yá'ąąshdi nááts'íílid tsíłkęęh.... Yá'ąąshdi nááts'íílid ch'ikęęh....

K'oslátah sidilts'įhí ii'ni' diłhił tsiłkęęh naat'áanii ii'ni' dootł'izh and

[68] When male prayersticks are used this order is followed, but for female prayersticks they alternate, that is *hakéédęę'* line is recited first, then *hatsiji'*.

[69] The beginning of the prayer is here noted for each prayerstick, male and female. The change, or "naming" the holy person to whom the stick is offered is indicated in the following. The patient may choose among these sets and the wording will be the same as that of the first prayer.

[70] That is, in female prayer to Water Horse, blue water is substituted for black water of the male Water Horse prayer. Then maiden is substituted for youth or young man, and alternations noted in note 68 must be observed in every prayer to the female prayerstick. To avoid useless repetition, the essential changes only have been noted.

ch'ikę́ęh and *ii'ni' łitso tsíłkę́ęh* and *ii'ni' łigai ch'ikę́ęh naat'áanii....*

K'os diłhił tsíłkę́ęh naat'áanii and *k'os dootł'izh ch'ikę́ęh naat'áanii.... Tó áłah náshchíín tsíłkę́ęh naat'áanii* and *tó biyáázh ch'ikę́ęh naat'áanii....*

Ni' ałníí' hooghangi ts'íís bi'áád tsíłkę́ęh naat'áanii and *ts'íís bi'áád ch'ikę́ęh naat'áanii....*

Dego hoolyéegi, dego hołk'áá' tsíłkę́ęh naat'áanii and *dego hoolyéegi, dego hołk'áá' ch'ikę́ęh naat'áanii....*

Táłtł'ááh náhálgaigi táłkáá' sidilts'įhí naal'eełí diłhiłii tsíłkę́ęh and *naal'eełí dootł'izhii ch'ikę́ę'.... Táłtł'ááh náhálgaigi naal'eełí doo naat'a'ígíí tsíłkę́ęh* and *ch'ikę́ęh naat'áanii....*

Tátł'ááh náhálgai tábąąh dighálí tábąąsdísítsoh tsíłkę́ęh and *ch'ikę́ęh naat'áanii.... Táłtł'ááh náhálgaigi tábąąsdísítsósí tsíłkę́ęh* and *ch'ikę́ęh naat'áanii....*

Tátł'ááh náhálgaigi tábąąh dighálí daak'įį' tsíłkę́ęh and *ch'ikę́ęh naat'áanii.... Táłtł'ááh náhálgaigi tákáá' dighálí yá'azhjool tsíłkę́ęh* and *ch'ikę́ęh naat'áanii....*

T'áłtł'ááh náhálgaigi tooji noołna' tsíłkę́ęh and *ch'ikę́ęh naat'áanii.... Táłtł'ááh náhálgaigi tooji ndiigai tsíłkę́ęh* and *ch'ikę́ęh.... Tátł'ááh náhálgaigi tooji náhábił tsíłkę́ęh* and *ch'ikę́ęh.... Táłtł'ááh náhálgaigi hoz tsíłkę́ęh* and *ch'ikę́ęh....*

Dził tánίί' siláagi tádiłhił bee dah honíkáągi tádiłhił yee sidáhí tsíłkę́ęh and *dził tánίί' naazláagi tádootł'izh bee dah honíkáągi dláád dootł'izh yee sidáhí ch'ikę́ęh naat'áanii....*

Tádiłhił bee hooghangi tádiłhił bee dahoníkáągi ch'ał nineezí tsíłkę́ęh and *tádootł'izh bee hooghangi tádootł'izh bee dah honíkáągi ch'ał nineezí ch'ikę́ęh naat'áanii....*

Táłtł'ááh náhálgaigi wónaalts'ílí tsíłkę́ę́h and *ch'ikę́ę́h*.... *Táłtł'ááh náhálgaigi ts'ǫǫ sání tsíłkę́ę́h* and *ch'ikę́ę́h naat'áanii*....

Nání'áigi tábąąstíín tsíłkę́ęh and *ch'ikę́ę́h naat'áanii*.... *Nání'áigi chaa' tsíłkę́ę́h* and *ch'ikę́ę́h naat'áanii*....

Táłtł'ááh náhálgaigi tsisteeł tsíłkę́ę́h and *ch'ikę́ę́h naat'áanii*.... *Táłtł'ááh náhálgaigi ch'ééh digháahii tsíłkę́ę́h* and *ch'ikę́ę́h*.... *Tó názbąsgi táłtł'ááh naaldoohí ts'ilgháán tsíłkę́ę́h* and *chikę́ę́h*.... *Táłtł'ááh náhálgaigi ch'ééh digháahii tsíłkę́ę́h* and *ch'ikę́ę́h*.... *Tó názbąsgi táłtł'ááh naaldoohí ts'ilgháán tsíłkę́ę́h* and *ch'ikę́ę́h*....

Be'ek'id hóteelígi tótł'iish tsíłkę́ę́h and *ch'ikę́ę́h*....

Ni' ałníí' hooghangi nahasdzáán bee dah honíkąąįgi nihazę́ęs yik'i dah sitíní na'ashǫ́'ii dich'ízhí tsíłkę́ę́h and *ch'ikę́ę́h*....

Ni' ałníí' hooghangi nahasdzáán bee bighaní nahasdzáán bee dah honíkąąįgi na'atł'oh diłhił tsíłkę́ę́h naat'áanii and *na'atł'oh dootł'izh ch'ikę́ę́h naat'áanii niyeel*....

Tsé diłhił bee bighaní tsé diłhił bee dah honíkąąįgi tsé naalch'óshii tsíłkę́ę́h and *ch'ikę́ę́h naat'áanii*....

Dah hoogaigi k'aalógiiłgai tsíłkę́ę́h naat'áanii and *ch'ikę́ę́h*....

27. K'eet'áán yáłti'í

151. K'eet'áán yáłti'í éí t'óó bikéé' adaaz'á. Éí doo bá yáti' da. Lók'aa' t'éí áł'į, ts'ídá t'áá át'é. K'eet'áán yáłti'ígíí naaki ílį. K'ai dootł'izh ál'į. Éí ádingo k'aiłchíí' ál'į. K'eet'áán yáłti'ígíí ahąąh njiléeh, nishtł'ají biką'ii, nish'náájí bi'áadii. Biką'ii diłhił; binii' dootł'izh. Bináá' hólǫ, bizéé' dó'. Bitáá' dzígai, biyaadáá' dzítso, bitá'ízh-dootł'izh.[71] Bi'áadii dootł'izh, binii' t'áá dootł'izh. Bináá' hólǫ, bizéé' dó'. Bitáá' dzígai, biyaadáá' dzitso bitá'ízhdiłhił. Biyaagi ats'os łigai njiiléeh. Bikáa'gi tązhiits'os njiiléeh. Áádóó índa tł'óh'azóół bee dįį'go bik'ézt'ingo dego hanáát'i'.

152. Ts'ídá ałtso táá' bik'ee ánííłtso, t'áá hazhó'ó k'eet'áán yáłti'ígíí t'éí atis ánííłtso łeeh daaz'áa doojį' háádahashjéé'. Índa díí ch'ał bik'eet'ánígíí t'éí ch'ałdąą' béstłéé'. Áádóó éí tsídá ałtso tółchiin béstłéé'.

[71] Instead of *bitsiit'áá'*, the top of its head.

28. Nihe'níiłgi

153. Nihe'níiłgi t'áá ałtso t'áá shá bik'ehgo t'éí nihe'níił. T'áá ákót'éego t'éí ałkéé' nihindééh. Díí tééhołtsódii lá, índa téélįį' bik'eet'ą' be'ek'id haz'ą́ąjį' nihe'níił. Níłtsą́ ashkii, níłtsą́ at'ééd hajilgish. Nááts'íílid bik'eet'ą' tó háálį́įjį' nihe'níił. Tó áłah náshchíín, tó biyáázh, níłtsą́ biką', níłtsą́ bi'áád tó háálį́įjį'. Éí ádingo t'óó hodees'éeljį' nihe'níił. Ii'ni' bik'eet'ą'ígíí, éí t'áá ó'oos'ni'jį' nihe'níił. Ts'ídá ałtso ch'il dilyésii biyaa shijéé'. Tótł'iish bik'eet'ą'ígíí éí díwózhiiłbáii biyaajį' sinil. Dego hołk'ąą' bik'eet'ą' tabąąhjį', éí doodago k'ai bich'į' sinil. Naat'a'gi bik'eet'ą'ígíí ts'ídá t'áá ałtso be'ek'id haz'ą́ąjį' sinil. Ch'ałígíí bik'eet'ą' tó deezlį́įjį', éí doodago haał'éeljį' sinil. Wónaalch'ilí ts'ǫǫ sání bił tséedis haz'ą́ągi łeezh shijaa'jį' sinil. Éí ádingo be'ek'id haz'ą́ąjį' sinil.

154. Be'ek'idígíí tó siyį́įgo na'aldloosh yii' náhoojahii doo ál'įį da. Háálá yik'i naaskaigo sits'ilgo báhádzid. Ńláahjí bik'i hojitaałii bohidizhdoołt'ih índa hójí dǫ́'. Éí bąą tó ádingo t'éiyá. Tábąąstíín, chaa', dzisteeł[72] índa ch'ééh digháahii bik'eet'ą'ígíí t'áá be'ek'id haz'ą́ąjį' náánás'nil. Ts'ilgháhígíí tótł'ishígíí tó siyį́įgo doo bich'į' na'adáajį' sinil. Éí doodago t'áá be'ek'id haz'ą́ąjį'. Na'ashǫ́'ii dich'ízhiígíí nahazęęs bich'į' sinil. Na'ashjé'ígíí t'áá bighanjį'. Éí doodago t'óó na'aztł'ǫ́ǫjį' bich'į' sinil. Tsé naalch'óshiígíí t'áá ałtso bighan bich'į' sinil. Éí doodago t'óó tsé bich'į' sinil. Tsé t'áá háát'i'ígíí éí doo ál'įį da. K'aalógiiłgai éí t'áá honíłteelgi ahíhoneel'ą́ąjį' sinil.

[72] *Tsisteeł* and *ch'ééh digháahii* are considered identical by some. Some pronounce *dzisteeł.*

155. Hózhǫ́ǫgo náádizhdoodááł, doo hąąh tééhgóó njigháa doo. Doo hohodééłníígóó njigháa doo.
Hatsiįį' hózhǫ́ǫgo njigháa doo. Hakéédęę' hózhǫ́ǫgo njigháa doo. Hayaagi hózhǫ́ǫgo njigháa doo. Hak'igi hózhǫ́ǫgo njigháa doo. Hanaa t'áá ałtso hózhǫ́ǫgo njigháa doo. Hazaa hahóózhǫǫdgo njigháa doo.
Są'ah naagháí bik'eh hózhóón jílį́įgo njigháa doo.
Hózhǫ́ náhásdlį́į́', dį́į'di (four times).

156. Ałtso náájiiłnihgo ákójiniih, t'áá áko dah nízhdiilwo'. K'eet'áán jookáałgo diné ła' hadááh yigháahgo doo bich'į' yájíłti' da. Hach'į' haadziih ndi doo bich'į' yájíłti' da. K'eet'ánígíí náhániihgóó yikáałgo ła' sits'ilgo doo t'áá ákót'éego nahidooniih da.[73] T'áá áko ndookáałii háádidoolnííł. Áko índa nahidooniih.

157. Díí k'eet'ánígíí diné bił nilį́įgo ts'ídá ałtso yiyah ni'iiléeh, bikáá' hadadilne'. Éí ńléí naak'aat'ąhí da, éí doodago béeso naaki yáál dó' hodees'áago t'áá'łá'í béesojį' nihool'á. Jó nihí dinéjígo bidáahjį' dadzitsaahgo hójóki'go, shiyiin doo, jiniihgo hoł ch'íjí'áahgo bee hahozhniłnééh. Aadóó hayiingo ch'íjígháahgo bee ha'iideeł. Dį́į'di bee hahojiłnééh. Aadóó índa t'áá hó bee ák'ijidláahgo hodilzhish. Áko kojí ańdahazt'i'góó yę́ę doo hąąh ji'į́įgóó hoł ch'íjí'áahgo hodilzhish. Diné niidlį́įjí hatáál nihá niilyáii ákót'éego baa yiikah. Éí bąą, są'ah naagháí bik'eh hózhóón át'é, dadii'ní. Éí bine' niit'į́įł. Áko lá át'é ni, shicheii.

[73]Low-toned *na* is permissible. Both low- and high-toned *ná* are used, *nahidooniih* and *náhidooniih*.

APPENDIX

Appendix

by Karl W. Luckert

The Editor's Perspective

Waterway in the present Navajo repertoire is an extremely reduced and in most localities even an extinct ceremonial tradition. It has been described so by Father Berard already in 1932, shortly after recording this chantway myth. This editor has come across a few fragments of Waterway ideology during his own work in the field, and they seem rather insignificant. Nevertheless, he might be forgiven if he uses these small hints from his own findings as first steps to a broader understanding of Water-person's power and his habits of interacting with the Navajo people.

The ontological link between *ajiłee* and Waterway was substantiated by Claus Chee Sonny in 1977, when he identified the hero of Slim Curly's *ajiłee* myth as Tumbling Waterdrop or as Waterdrop Boy (Luckert, 1978, pp. 180ff.). According to Claus Chee Sonny, Water or Moisture gives life, and in the exuberance of sexual passion the procreation of new life in moisture is accompanied by a certain measure of *ajiłee* craziness. This is one of the phenomena by which the excessive power of Water becomes manifest. In his introduction, above, Father Berard mentions this dimension even more precisely: "originally, venereal and skin diseases must have sought relief in this ceremony." This would suggest that a kind of Waterway ceremonial was formerly called for when *ajiłee* symptoms had progressed to more serious venereal disorders.

Another dimension of the Waterway tradition points to Rain ceremonialism. This appears to have been relevant especially in the more arid Kayenta and Navajo Mountain area. Certain marginal statements which in that area were made by informants concerning the life-giving and destructive powers of Water (Luckert, 1977), come now into clearer focus in relation to Waterway. The shift of emphasis from healing to Rain ceremonialism becomes quite obvious when one peruses materials that were collected by researchers other than Father Berard.

The overall fragmented state of the available Waterway materials does not permit presentation of a coherent synthesis here. What can be done, at most, is to refer to the available fragments and to point the reader to research that must be hoped for in the future.

Waterway Mythology

It is perhaps significant that the bulk of Waterway materials does come from the 1930s, and that after that decade the sources seem to have dried up. This may indicate the demise of an already weakened tradition, brought about when established Waterway and Rainway singers died without leaving behind fully trained successors. This state of affairs is reflected in the recently documented decline of Navajo Mountain and Rainbow Bridge rain ceremonialism (see Luckert, 1977, pp. 27ff.). But surely, Navajo thinking about Rain and Water did not cease that suddenly in the late 1930s. The decline in interest in religious and mythic subject matters, among scientific anthropologists, seems to be responsible for at least part of the subsequent scarcity of information.

Dane and Mary Coolidge published in 1930 a general volume on *The Navaho Indians*. In it they mentioned the myth of a Rain ceremony (p. 86.). The Great Gambler episode and the seduction of the two Raingod wives, themes which the Coolidges mention, might well at one time have enhanced the present Father Berard version.

In the Frances Gillmor and Louisa Wetherill book, *Traders to the Navajos* (1934, pp. 112-23), Rainway and Waterway mythology flows more freely in the form of a Deer Water People clan myth. The myth of emergence, which for many Navajo ceremonial traditions has become ontological bedrock, is here also laid down to explain the origin and to establish the efficacy of Water-related ceremonial practices. Leland C. Wyman, in *The Sandpaintings of the Kayenta Navaho* (1952, pp. 24ff.) has condensed this myth and has presented it together with descriptions and drawings of the seven Waterway sandpaintings in the Wetherill collection.

Two Waterway myths were published in 1946 by Mary C. Wheelwright in *Hail Chant and Water Chant*. The first of these came from "Hasteen B'Gohdi," who lived near Winslow; it was told to the author by a certain "Big Mustache" at Crystal in October 1933. The second version was given by "Klahzhin Begay" and by his younger brother "Klahzhin Betsilli" in 1937. During November of 1937 Mary Wheelwright also obtained from "Klahzhin" an outline of Waterway procedures. The two Wheelwright versions, together with Father Berard's manuscript published herein, have been nicely abstracted by Katherine Spencer in her inimitable work on Navajo *Mythology and Values* (1957, 107ff.).

To this scanty list of Waterway materials the "American Tribal Religions" series is now able to add Father Berard's full bilingual recording of Black Mustache Circle's narration. The important task of harmonizing the entire scope of Waterway mythology thematically, and the placement of these themes in the context of Navajo ceremonial history, must be left to students of the future. The immediate task of this monograph series is to make primary source materials available and to rescue what still can be found as quickly as possible from oblivion.

The Sandpaintings of Rain- and Waterway

Fourteen Rain- and Waterway sandpaintings could be located by the time this volume was being readied for printing. Four of these have been published previously, in color, in Mary Wheelwright's *Hail Chant and Water Chant* (pp. 194-201). They are reprinted here in black-and-white with permission of the Wheelwright Museum at Santa Fe. One fairly certain, and two probable Waterway sandpaintings from singer Fur-hat, were collected and redrawn by Franc Johnson Newcomb; drawings of two wooden tablets belonging to Waterway have also been found. These, too, can be included here through the generosity of the Wheelwright Museum. Our special gratitude is expressed to Susan McGreevey, director of the Museum. Seven additional sandpainting reproductions are from the Wetherill collection and are included in this volume by courtesy of the Museum of Northern Arizona. Descriptions of these sandpaintings, and drawings, have already been published by Leland C. Wyman in 1952.

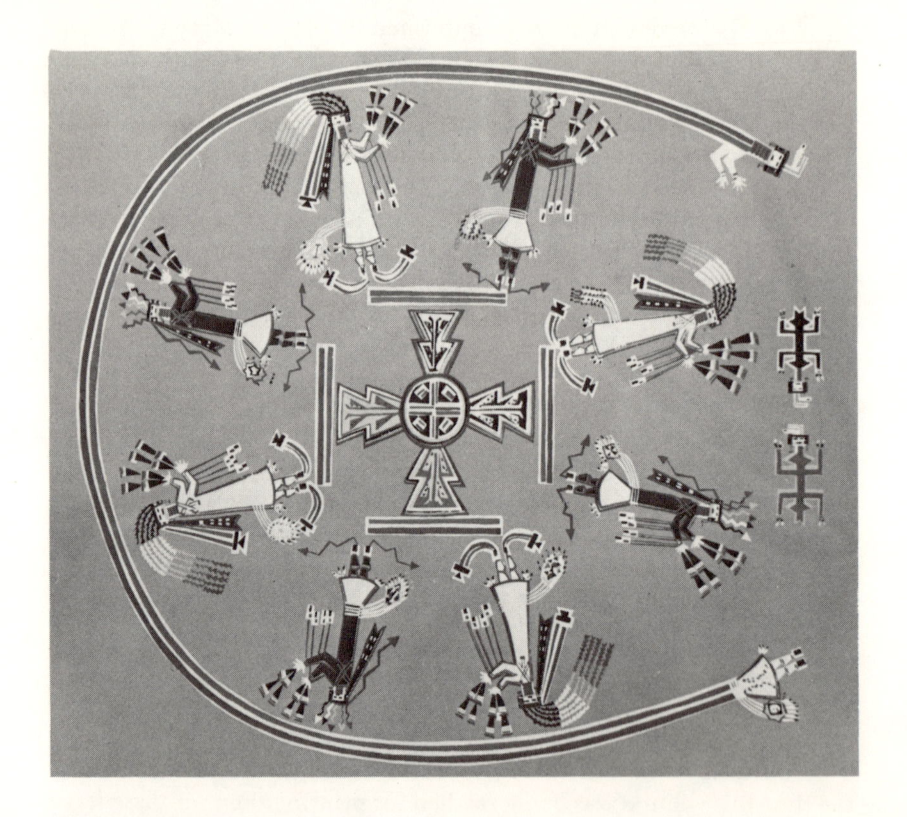

Sandpainting 1

The central Water is surrounded by four cloud symbols with dragonflies on them. Around these are four rainbow bars. The eight Holy Water People (Rain Boys and Rain Girls) hold "held-to-water" plumes in their hands. The female figures, in white, have black rain-hair and rainbow hanging from their heads, and long curved feathered headdresses in five colors. They travel on rainbow arcs tipped with cloud symbols. The male figures, in black, have black rain-hair and red lightning hanging from their heads, and headdresses of five lightning darts. They travel on red lightning. The painting is surrounded by the Rainbow, and the guardians at the east are two "Dontsos," the Messenger Flies.

The name of the singer is not given for sandpaintings 1 through 4, but he may have been Black's Son from Tsebitoh, Arizona, who learned from Hastiin B'Gohdi of Bitahotchee, near Winslow (Note by Leland C. Wyman). Illustration by Franc Johnson Newcomb (1937), in Mary C. Wheelwright, *Hail Chant and Water Chant,* p. 195; description adopted from p. 194. Santa Fe, 1946. Courtesy of the Wheelwright Museum, Santa Fe.

Sandpainting 2

This sandpainting is similar to the first, but it includes the four sacred plants—corn, beans, squash, tobacco. The Rain People all travel on rainbow arcs tipped with black cloud symbols. The guardians in the east are "Dontsos."

Illustration by Franc Johnson Newcomb (1937), in Mary C. Wheelwright, *Hail Chant and Water Chant,* p. 197; description adopted from p. 196. Santa Fe, 1946. Courtesy of the Wheelwright Museum, Santa Fe.

Sandpainting 3

This is a sandpainting of the Water Monsters who figure in the Waterway myth. The center of the picture is similar to that of the second painting—with central water, cloud symbols, rainbow bars, and the four sacred plants—except that above the corn in this painting is Bluebird. The four Water Monsters have black clouds on their heads, and their legs end in cloud symbols. The eastern opening of the surrounding Rainbow is protected by a brown Otter and a black Beaver. Their legs also end in black cloud symbols.

Illustration by Franc Johnson Newcomb (1937), in Mary C. Wheelwright, *Hail Chant and Water Chant,* p. 199; description adopted from p. 198. Santa Fe, 1946. Courtesy of the Wheelwright Museum, Santa Fe.

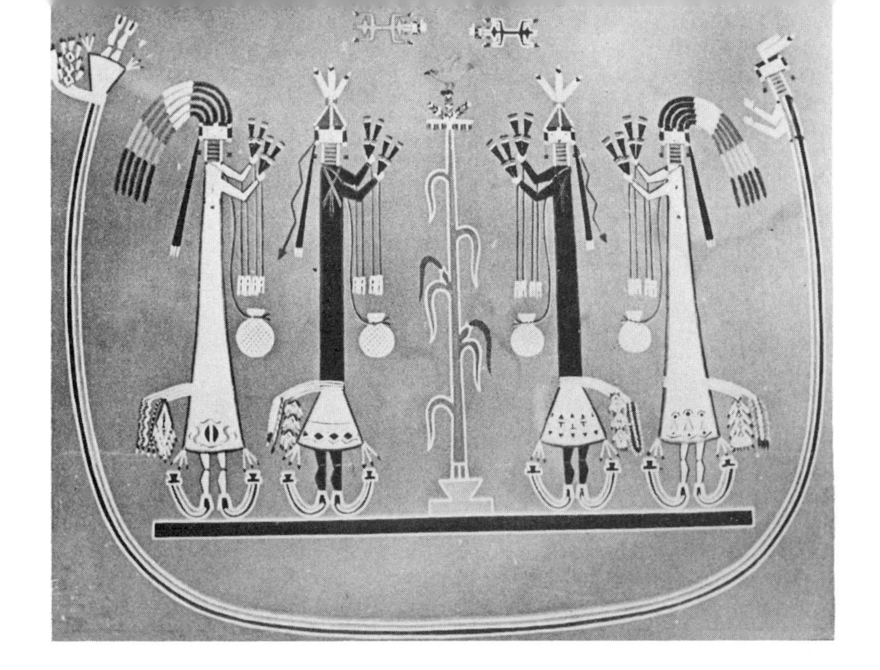

Sandpainting 4

The notes which come with this sandpainting refer to four female figures, but similar figures in sandpaintings 1 and 2 have been identified as male and female rain personages. The Rain People in this sandpainting face the blue corn at the center and bring rain to it. They carry black "held-to-water" plumed wands and blue water bottles in white wicker-work. The deities have straight black rain-hair and stand on curved rainbows that have black clouds at their tips. The males are represented with black bodies, the females wear white dresses; the males wear pointed hats with three eagle feathers, and the females have headdresses of five black-white-red feathers.

Painting by Franc Johnson Newcomb (1937), by courtesy of the Wheelwright Museum, Santa Fe. Note based on information by Leland C. Wyman.

In addition to a series of Waterway prayersticks, the collection contains drawings on two wooden tablets—a functional synthesis of prayer feathers and painted *ye'ii*-figures. The first and second drawings, on the front and back of the first tablet, show Rainboy; the third and fourth drawings, on the second tablet, show Raingirl. Courtesy of the Wheelwright Museum, Santa Fe.

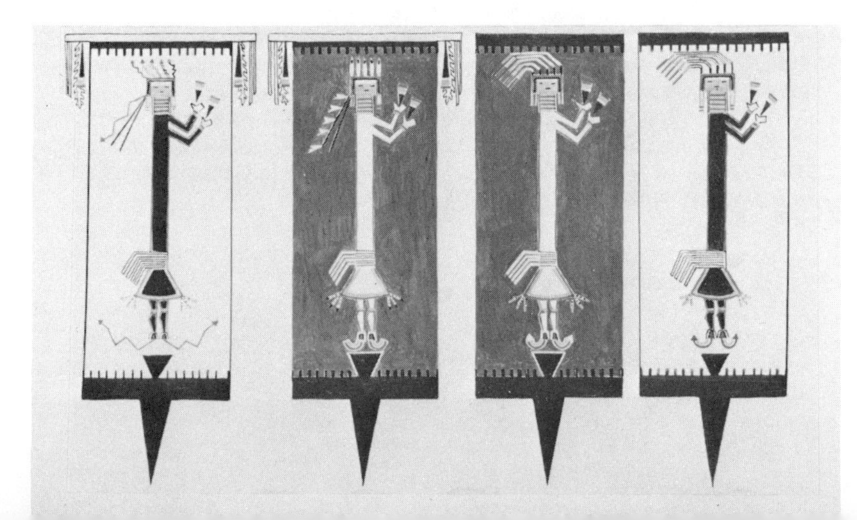

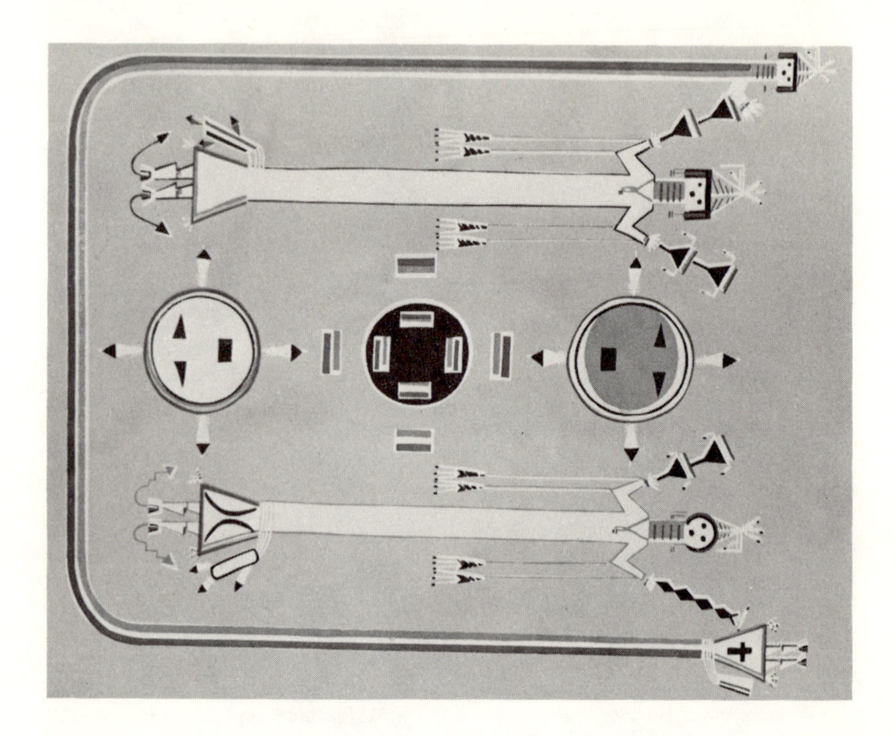

Sandpainting 5

This sandpainting shows two dancers performing the corral dance ("fire dance") phase of a nine-night ceremonial, a specialty of Waterway. In the dance the impersonator of the male, with yellow body and round face, has the blue Sun strapped to his shoulders; the impersonator of the female, with white body and square face, has the white Moon strapped on his shoulders. In the sandpainting, the male figure stands on crooked blue lightning arrows; he holds a double black "held-to-water" plumed wand and a flash of lightning. The female figure stands on curved (straight) black lightning arrows, she carries "held-to-water" plumed wands in both hands. During the sandpainting rite, a male patient sits on the black dark-circle-of-branches at the center; a female patient sits on the Moon which for her is painted in the center of the sandpainting. This is the only sandpainting used in that particular rite and such rites are rare.

The singer is given as "At-the-Junction-of-the-Rivers." Illustration by Laura A. Armer (1929?), in Mary C. Wheelwright, *Hail Chant and Water Chant*, p. 201. Santa Fe, 1946. Courtesy of the Wheelwright Museum, Santa Fe. Note based on information by Leland C. Wyman.

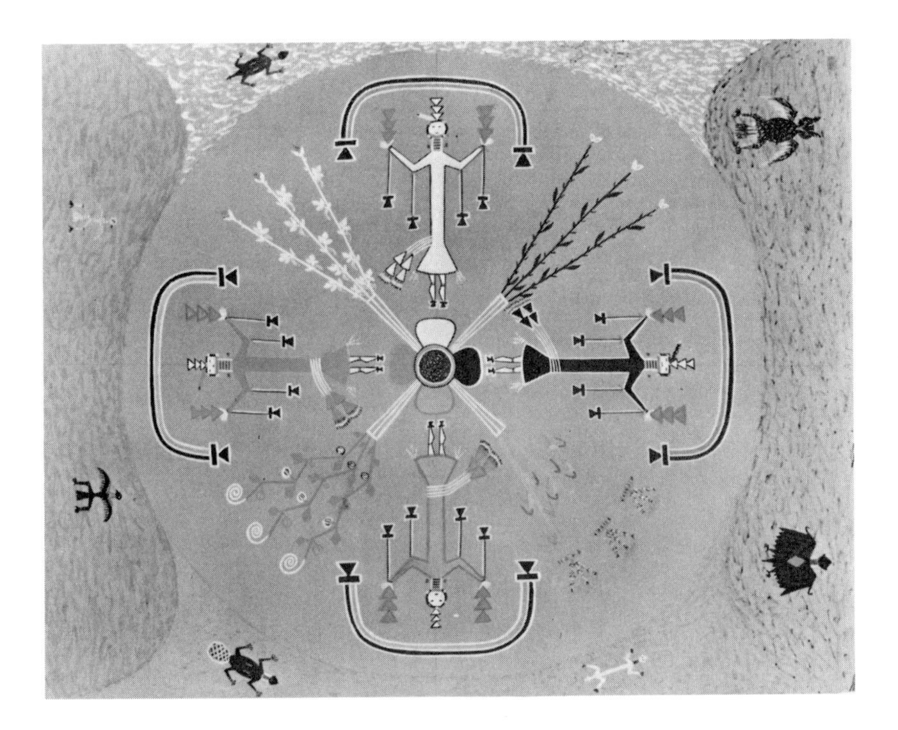

Sandpainting 6

This sandpainting was made by the singer Fur-hat at Newcomb in 1935. The name of the ceremony is not known, but it could have been a Water chant; or, it could have been a Wind ceremony for rain. The center is the bottomless lake on a mountain top, surrounded by four clouds. The roots of the four sacred Mountains spring from the lake. Four Rain people stand in the four directions carrying clouds in their hands and on their heads. Their feet and medicine bundles are clouds-meeting-earth. They wear the white masks of the Water and Hail people. Over each head bends a rainbow arc, also ending in clouds-meeting-earth. In the spreading mists around the central portion of the design are Owl and Bat (east), Blackbird and Martin (west), Beaver and Salamander (south), and Otter and Salamander (north).

Painting and note by Franc Johnson Newcomb. Courtesy of the Wheelwright Museum, Santa Fe.

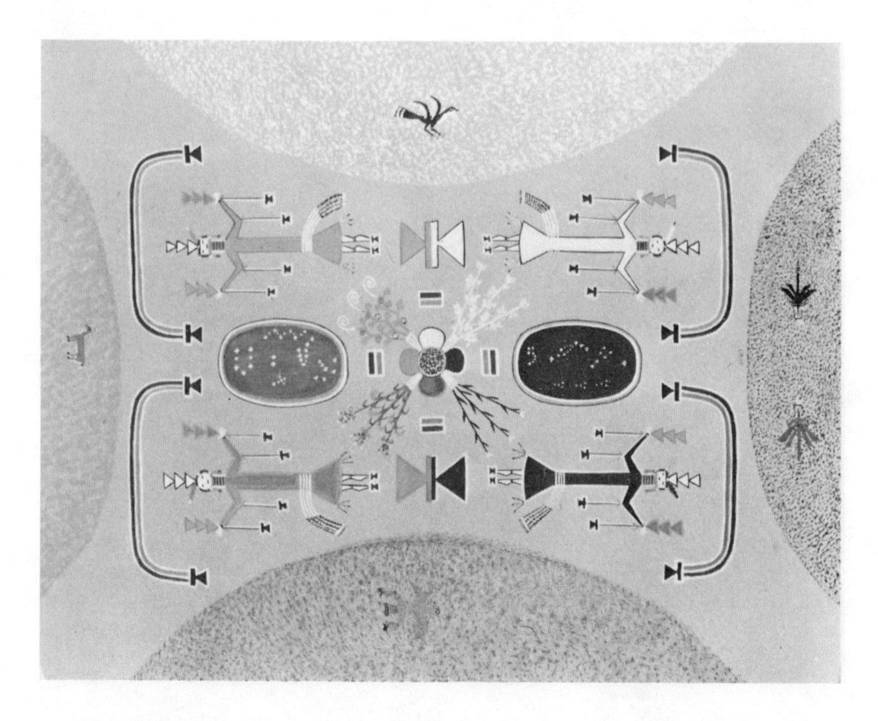

Sandpainting 7

This is the second-day sandpainting of a Rain ceremony by the singer Fur-hat. In the center is the emergence lake, sprinkled with various kinds of pollen and with four plants that were brought up from the lower world. There are four rainbow spots. Two large bodies of water, probably the eastern and western oceans, reflect constellations of stars. Double clouds-meeting-earth, on each side, indicate mountain tops on which the Rain (i.e. Cloud) People stand. They are carrying the clouds. Mists surround this painting. There are two Dragon-flies in the east, a Mountain-goat in the west, a Flicker in the south—it drums for rain, and a Magpie in the north—it carries the rain on its tail. There were two more paintings to this set, but the singer did not come back to the Trading Post that fall of 1935, and in the winter he died.

Painting and note by Franc Johnson Newcomb. Courtesy of the Wheel-wright Museum, Santa Fe.

Sandpainting 8

The original was done in crayon, pencil, white paint; cloth backed, pale tan drawing paper. There are no notes. *Center:* black, white spots; yellow, blue, and red outlines; heart-shaped white and tridigitate yellow points. *Sides:* plants, yellow branches and stem; blue-green leaves; red, yellow, and blue-green flowers; red-black bird with blue and red shoulder and yellow neck. *Corners:* white people; yellow forearms and lower legs bearing blue zigzag lightnings; white faces; blue bird on head; three red and two blue zigzag lightning arrows in each hand; standing on sundogs.

Note after Leland C. Wyman, *The Sandpaintings of the Kayenta Navaho,* p. 26. Albuquerque, 1952. Photograph by courtesy of the Museum of Northern Arizona.

Sandpainting 9

The original was done in crayon; cloth backed, pale tan drawing paper. "Second day." *Center:* black lines on yellow backgrounds, red-black cloud symbols with yellow outlines. *Sides:* plants, green branches; green leaves; flowers, red-brown center, yellow, red, and green petals; yellow roots ("flowers of the land of the Water clan people"). *Corners:* blue people, yellow forearms and lower legs, blue feet, uncolored faces; red hat with yellow, red, and blue fringe ("Coyote of the dark land, chief of the people from the dark land").

Note after Leland C. Wyman, *The Sandpaintings of the Kayenta Navaho,* p. 28. Albuquerque, 1952. Photograph by courtesy of the Museum of Northern Arizona.

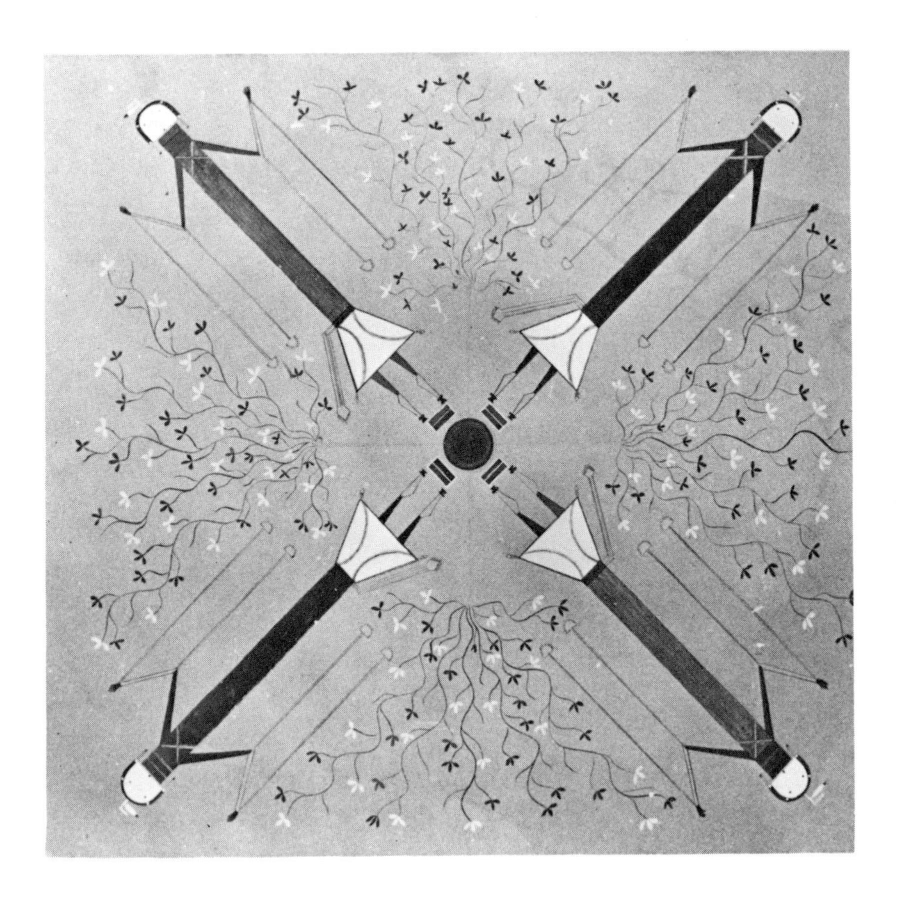

Sandpainting 10

The original was done in crayon, white paint; cloth backed, pale tan drawing paper. "Third day." *Center:* dark greenish-brown ("water"); dark green, red, and yellow outlines. *Sides:* plants, red, green, white, or yellow leaves; yellow roots. *Corners:* people, two dark blue-green opposite and two red-black opposite; yellow forearms and legs; white faces; standing on sundogs, red inside ("daughter of the spirits, the wife of Chief of the Water clan; the leader of the women; caused the trouble which drove the men from the island").

Note after Leland C. Wyman, *The Sandpaintings of the Kayenta Navaho,* p. 28. Albuquerque, 1952. Photograph by courtesy of the Museum of Northern Arizona.

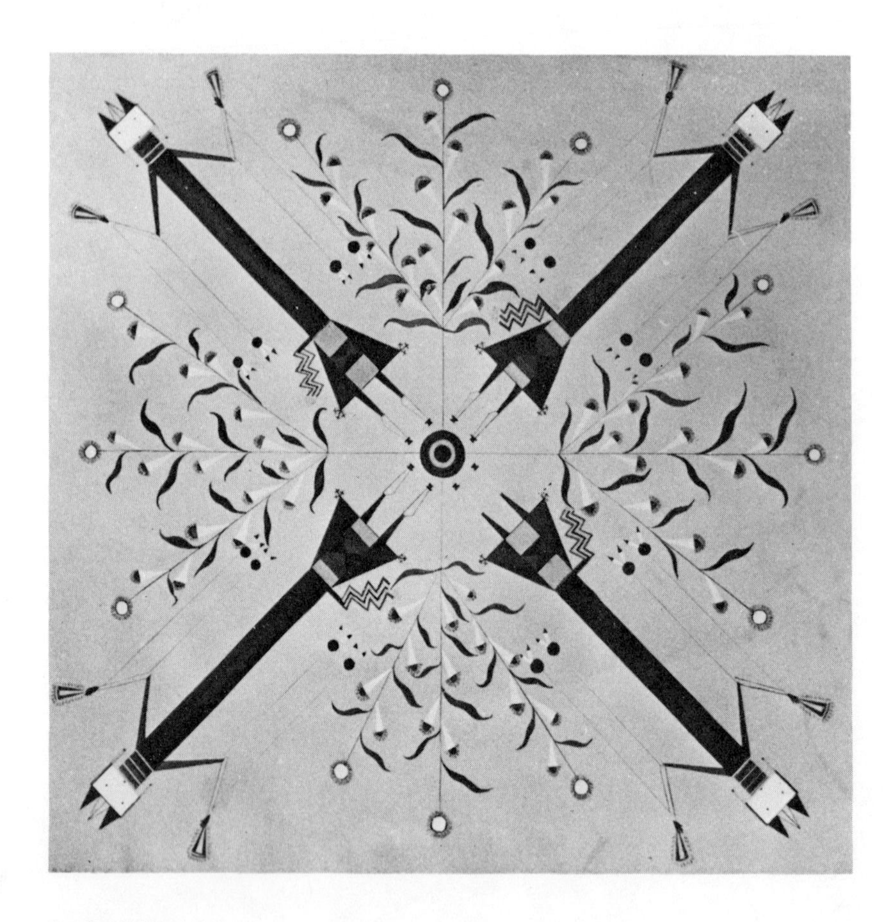

Sandpainting 11

The original was done in crayon, pencil, white paint; cloth backed, pale tan drawing paper. "Fourth day." *Center:* green; yellow, red, and blue outlines. *Sides:* plants, green leaves; terminal flowers, white center, black outline, red, green, and yellow petals; lateral flowers, white bottom, red top, red, blue, and yellow petals. *Corners:* red people; yellow forearms and lower legs; white faces; two green points with red outlines (outside) and a yellow point with black outline and center stripe (center) on head; yellow (center) and green (sides) "seed basket full of seeds," with red, blue, and yellow fringe, in each hand ("Coyote of the dark land. He was taken from the island with the Water clan people and carried the seeds").

Note after Leland C. Wyman, *The Sandpaintings of the Kayenta Navaho,* pp. 28, 30. Albuquerque, 1952. Photograph by courtesy of the Museum of Northern Arizona.

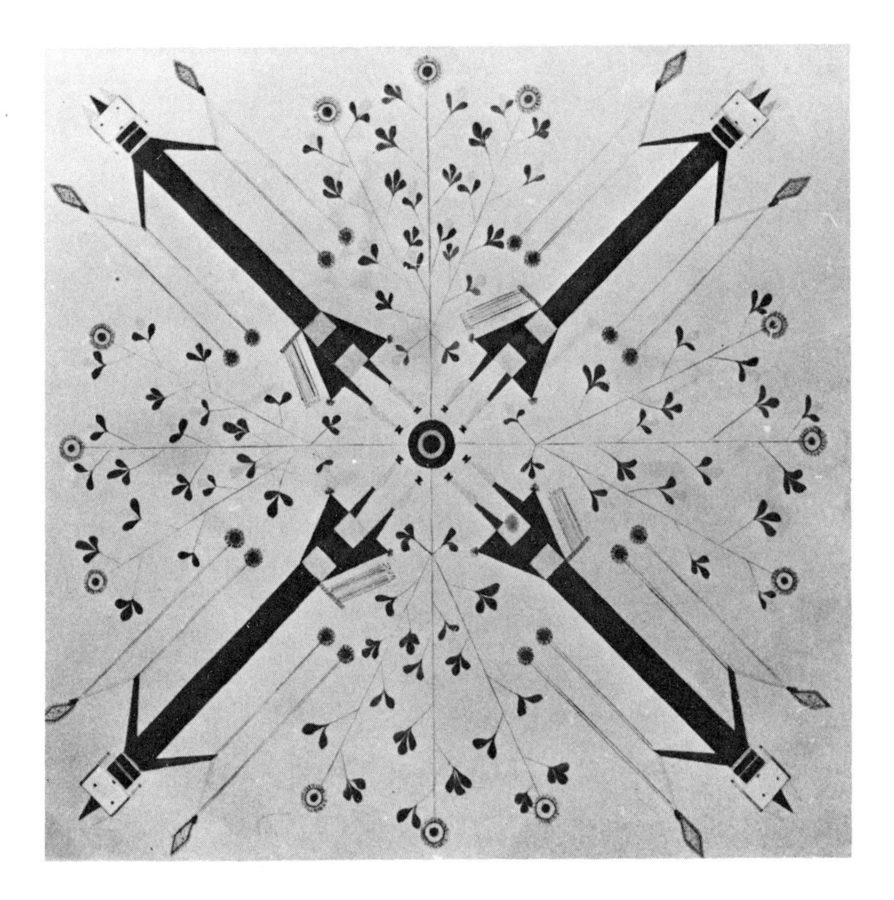

Sandpainting 12

The original was done in crayon, pencil; cloth backed, pale tan drawing paper. "Fifth day." *Center:* green; yellow, blue, and red outlines. *Sides:* plants, leaves with green outer and red or yellow center leaflets; flowers, green center, yellow, red, green and/or blue outlines and petals. *Corners:* red people; yellow forearms and lower legs; black feet; uncolored faces; two yellow (outside) and a red and blue (center) point on head; yellow "stone knives" with red and green serrations and dots in each hand ("Coyote of the dark land, the leader of the discontent which brought on the great flood and drought").

Note after Leland C. Wyman, *The Sandpaintings of the Kayenta Navaho,* p. 30. Albuquerque, 1952. Photograph by courtesy of the Museum of Northern Arizona.

Sandpainting 13

The original was done in crayon, white paint; cloth backed, pale tan drawing paper. "Sixth day." *Center:* black lines on red backgrounds and sundogs; small black outline square around the crossing. *Sides:* plants, green branches; green leaves; flowers, "heart shaped" yellow centers, thick black, red, and green outlines; black roots. *Corners:* white people, yellow forearms, black legs; uncolored faces; clouds, with yellow, green, blue and red segments; top segment with blue and red fringe; in each hand ("White Light of the Heavens, offering a prayer for rain").

Note after Leland C. Wyman, *The Sandpaintings of the Kayenta Navaho*, p. 30. Albuquerque, 1952. Photograph by courtesy of the Museum of Northern Arizona.

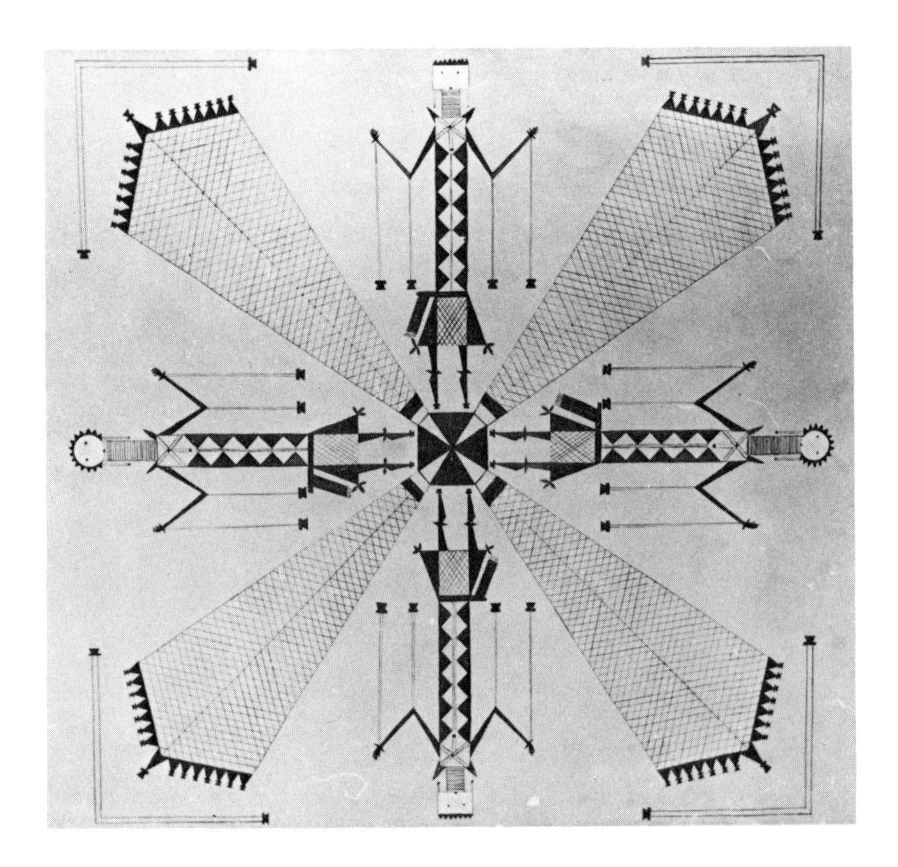

Sandpainting 14

The original was done in crayon, pencil; cloth backed, pale tan drawing paper. "Seventh day." The entire picture, with exceptions noted below, is in red and blue (or purple) crayon; red and blue lines alternate; triangular points are red with blue outlines. Feet, hands, and features are black. *Center:* red with yellow corner triangles, blue outlines ("The clouds which the god and goddess of lightning have kept from the people, representing the time of the great drought"). *Sides:* people, two with round heads ("god of lightning"), two with square heads ("goddess of lightning"); flint point armor; they "carry the rain and lightning buttoned in their clothes." *Corners:* "the seed baskets of the heavens with the seeds of the earth securely tied up."

Note after Leland C. Wyman, *The Sandpaintings of the Kayenta Navaho,* pp. 30, 32. Albuquerque, 1952. Photograph by courtesy of the Museum of Northern Arizona.

REFERENCES CITED IN THE APPENDIX

Coolidge, Dane and Mary R. Coolidge
1930 *The Navaho Indians.* Boston.

Gillmor, Frances and Louisa Wade Wetherill
1934 *Traders to the Navajos.* Cambridge.

Luckert, Karl W.
1977 *Navajo Mountain and Rainbow Bridge Religion.* American Tribal Religions, vol. 1. Flagstaff.
1978 *A Navajo Bringing-Home Ceremony, the Claus Chee Sonny Version of Deerway* ajiłee. American Tribal Religions, vol. 3. Flagstaff.

Spencer, Katherine
1957 *Mythology and Values, an Analysis of Navaho Chantway Myths.* Memoirs of the American Folklore Society, vol. 48. Philadelphia.

Wheelwright, Mary C.
1946 *Hail Chant and Water Chant.* Museum of Navajo Ceremonial Art, Santa Fe.

Wyman, Leland C.
1952 *The Sandpaintings of the Kayenta Navaho, an Analysis of the Louisa Wade Wetherill Collection.* University of New Mexico Publications in Anthropology, vol. 7. Albuquerque.

ACKNOWLEDGMENTS

Permission to print was given by the Franciscan Missionary Union, by the Museum of Northern Arizona, and by the University of Arizona Special Collections Library. Irvy Goossen has transcribed Father Berard's Navajo texts into current orthography. Katherine Bartlett has assisted in locating source materials, and Mark Middleton has restored old and marginal photographs for our use. Judith Hart has helped in the task of proofreading the English text. Rick Stetter, Gary McClellan and Steve Gustafson have assisted in various steps along the way. Lufa-type of Flagstaff has done the composition, and Classic Printers of Prescott have seen the book through to its completion.

AMERICAN TRIBAL RELIGIONS

Volume 1. *NAVAJO MOUNTAIN AND RAINBOW BRIDGE RELIGION*, 1977.
Karl W. Luckert

Volume 2. *LOVE-MAGIC AND BUTTERFLY PEOPLE: THE SLIM CURLY VERSION OF THE AJIŁEE AND MOTHWAY MYTHS*, 1978.
Father Berard Haile, O.F.M.

Volume 3. *A NAVAJO BRINGING-HOME CEREMONY: THE CLAUS CHEE SONNY VERSION OF DEERWAY AJIŁEE*, 1978.
Karl W. Luckert

Volume 4. *RAINHOUSE AND OCEAN: SPEECHES FOR THE PAPAGO YEAR*, 1979.
Ruth M. Underhill, Donald M. Bahr, Baptisto Lopez, Jose Pancho, David Lopez

Volume 5. *WATERWAY: A NAVAJO CEREMONIAL MYTH TOLD BY BLACK MUSTACHE CIRCLE*, 1979.
Father Berard Haile, O.F.M.

Supplement 1. *MOTHER EARTH ONCE WAS A GIRL: A SCIENTIFIC THEORY ON THE EXPANSION OF PLANET EARTH*, 1979.
Karl W. Luckert